THE
LITTLE GIANT®
ENCYCLOPEDIA
OF
Wedding Toasts

D0668584

Sterling Publishing Co., Inc.
New York

Compiled by David Macfarlane
Book design by Laura Best

The author has strived to be as accurate as possible with
the exact wording of direct quotes and with attribution to
original source. Our apologies in advance for any misrepre-
sentation or inaccuracy due to the reprinting of sources.

Library of Congress Cataloging-in-Publication Data Available

10 9 8 7 6 5 4 3 2 1

Published by Sterling Publishing Company, Inc.
387 Park Avenue South, New York, N.Y. 10016
©2000 by Sterling Publishing Co., Inc.
Distributed in Canada by Sterling Publishing
℅ Canadian Manda Group, One Atlantic Avenue, Suite 105
Toronto, Ontario, Canada M6K 3E7
Distributed in Great Britain and Europe by Cassell PLC
Wellington House, 125 Strand, London WC2R 0BB, England
Distributed in Australia by Capricorn Link (Australia) Pty Ltd.
P.O. Box 6651, Baulkham Hills, Business Centre,
NSW 2153, Australia

Printed in Canada

Sterling ISBN 0-8069-4175-8

Foreword

For the bride and groom, their wedding day will undoubtedly be the best day of their lives, marked by close friends, family members, ceremony, emotion, joy, good food, amusing stories, and a precious future to look forward to.

You will probably have a good time as well, but at some point near the end of the ceremony, as the rings are being exchanged and the minister makes his pronouncements, you may start to feel a bit uneasy. You probably won't even notice the anxiety at first, but by the time half the guests have left the buffet line and are diving into the prime rib, you could be having a full-blown panic attack.

If this is true, then you must have some sort of role to play in this blessed event. Regardless of whether you are the bride, bridegroom, best man, father of the bride, maid of honor, third cousin once removed from Wichita, or the hired bartender, the honor of your participation carries with it a little responsibility.

If this is even a semitraditional affair, YOU may have to make a speech. Now, the first thing to remember is that the best way to handle a little nervousness associated with having to say a few words is NOT to head to the bar and order a vat of martinis. People cannot understand you when you slur.

Instead, invest a little time in some preparation, put some words down on paper if you need to, and enable your personality with a little confidence. The key is to be exactly the person who was so honored by the bride and groom as to be included in the ceremony, and not purely the master of ceremonies, a Las Vegas lounge act, or a stand-up comic.

Knowing what you are going to say beforehand will make all the difference in the world. The purpose of this book is to arm you with the information you will need to sound witty, effervescent, and well-educated.

If you have purchased this book, you may be asking yourself, "Why make a wedding speech?" Well, the reasons are numerous, somewhat varied, and infinitely worthwhile. Your job may be to send the newlyweds off with the best wishes of all in attendance. It may be to impart wisdom to the bride and groom.

Who knows, your responsibility may be to let the guests know that this is not a clothing optional event. In the end, the real reason for making a toast or speech is because it is an honored custom. Of course, while it is possible to make a speech without including a toast and to make a toast without expanding it into a speech, at most weddings the two are simply combined.

Good thing! Your job just became half as difficult (or twice as easy, if you're an optimist.)

Contents

Who Gives What & Why

The reason that speeches and toasts are a part of wedding ceremonies is tradition, so it follows that the who and when of giving toasts and speeches would also be dictated by tradition. Having said that, keep in mind that the context of the wedding and the sensibilities of the participants will ultimately determine the comments made at any particular wedding.

Perhaps you will be the father of the bride, handsomely dressed in a designer tux and lifting a glass of Dom Perignon toward the rafters of the most grand cathedral in Chicago. Or, you might be planning to honor the happy couple with a wish that Gala bless their union as a small party of friends and family, dressed in nothing but wildflowers and standing in a remote mountain meadow, looks on in support. You will have to decide what is most appropriate based on the details of the event.

If you do wish to observe tradition, however, this is the commonly acknowledged order to follow:

Bride's Father/Old Family Friend—Either of these individuals (again, depending on the situation and who has given the bride away) will usually give the initial speech, and will conclude with a toast to the health of the bride and the bridegroom.

Response by the Bridegroom—The second speech is given as a reply to that of the father of the bride, and is the duty of the bridegroom. The bridegroom will want to conclude his remarks with a toast to the bridesmaids.

The Best Man Enters—Stepping to the fore at this point on behalf of the bridesmaids is the best man, who brings full circle the verbalization of honors by ending his speech with a toast to the parents of the bride and groom.

Should you follow these ceremonial dictates? That is a question only the organizer of the wedding can answer. In this day and age, wedding ceremonies often take on such individual and peculiar characteristics that categorizing them falls to those who have a perfect vision of what they want. Everyone else is left to just stand back and take it all in. If you know you are going to be participating in a wedding ceremony, either base your performance on what you know of the individuals getting married (if you know them

well), or ask what kind of ceremony it is going to be.
Better you determine exactly what will happen than
find out at the last minute that you have rented a tux
for a wedding with a Western theme. OOPS! Big
mistake, Tex!

Am I On Now?

In some instances, weddings are events timed as
carefully as a NASA launch. In other instances, the
ceremony can proceed at the leisurely pace of a
Mexican weekend. By now you should know which
one of these you are more likely to participate in, so
behave accordingly.

If the wedding reception is rather formal and includes
a lengthy seated dinner, speeches and toasts should
begin after all the guests have concluded their entire
meal. At very formal receptions, according to
tradition, the speeches are immediately preceded by
comments from the toastmaster, who announces,
"Ladies and gentlemen, you may now smoke!" Most
likely, this is not the wedding in which you will be a
participant, but whose to say. While most weddings
probably do not include the services of a toastmaster,
this is an issue we will briefly address later, for those
interested.

If the meal is to be concluded with tea or coffee and wedding cake, then speeches should proceed following the cutting of the cake. Again, as the coordinator of a wedding or anyone planning their own wedding, it is important to emphasize a sensitivity to the way in which the wedding is proceeding when deciding to break in and grab everyone's attention. If you can sense that the guests are full, slightly inebriated, and firmly planted in their chairs, then you probably have some leeway in deciding when to begin the speeches. If everyone is itching to get on the dance floor, you will need to pick the right moment when everyone is still loosely collected in order to get their attention.

Perhaps the wedding is an all-night affair. If so, the cutting of the cake can wait until speeches and toasts are made, after which the cake gets sliced up, the guests are served and everyone dances the night away in a joyous stupor! Remember, the sequence is quite alterable, and it is up to whoever is planning it to determine.

The Toastmaster—We can probably safely say that unless the bride and groom retain very strong ties to either the old country or British tradition, this will not be a part of the equation. But, for the sake of argument, let's say that it is. What a toastmaster offers is the opportunity for everyone who is participating in the wedding to be free from having to worry about overseeing and timing the social aspects of the event. Instead, the bride, bridegroom, and parents of each can more easily relax and simply enjoy the flow of the wedding as predetermined and as it is nurtured by someone else.

In specific terms, the responsibilities of the toastmaster include announcing guests in a receiving line, and asking the guests to be seated in anticipation of dinner being served (toastmasters are, after all, supposed to have loud voices and can better perform this function than the bride, who should avoid shouting on this particular day.) In addition, a toastmaster will be responsible for announcing grace as given by a member of the clergy, and for making the guests aware that it is time for the toasts and speeches to begin.

Traditionally, in the absence of a toastmaster to make certain the proceedings flow smoothly, this responsibility falls upon the best man.

Whatever will I say?

Virtually all of the remaining pages in this book will be dedicated to witicisms, expressions of thanks, axioms about love, maxims regarding life in general, and helpful phrases to get you through a wedding speech and/or toast. Yet those tidbits of philosophy and wisdom will not help you determine exactly what the subject of your comments should be, they will just make you sound like you know a great deal more about the subject than perhaps you do.

Of course, your comments will be directed at the participants in the wedding: the bride and bride-groom, the parents of the couple, the bridesmaids. This does not limit the subject of your comments to these people and no one else, but they are the objects of the days events, so why not give them the attention they deserve. While you may be able to stand up and keep half the audience in rapt attention by talking about the intricacies of hedge funds, that would be a bit inappropriate. You will naturally want to tailor your speech and/or toast to fit the personality of the person or people about which you are speaking, but following are some suggestions as to what each speaker might want to address in the course of their comments.

Bride's Father/Old Family Friend

As mentioned, if the father of the bride is absent for any reason, these comments should be made by whomever has given the bride away. Assuming the father of the bride is in attendance, then he will be making his initial comments not only as the bride's father but also as the host of the wedding. He will speak on behalf of his wife and himself and may want to address any or all of the following:

- a particular welcome to the groom's parents and family members from both sides, and a general welcome to all in attendance. Thanks to all who attended, particularly if the wedding has required lengthy travel for a number of the guests.

- the pride he and his wife feel for their daughter

- a funny or poignant story about events leading up to the wedding

- a tale from the bride's life to illustrate her personality and demeanor (in a positive manner)

- heartfelt congratulations to the groom and welcoming him into the family

- how much fun it has been getting to know the groom's family

- the trust you have in the newlyweds that their life together will be marvelous
- some words of wisdom for the young couple as they start life together
- a concluding toast "to the enduring health and happiness of the bride and groom"

The Bridegroom

The bridegroom speaks for both himself and his new wife. The purpose of his comments is to thank the numerous individuals who have been involved in making the wedding such a success. Other issues he might address include:

- thanks to the father of the bride for his toast
- thanks to the parents of his new wife for her hand, for raising such a remarkable woman, etc.
- appreciation for the wedding and the reception
- the honor it is to have been welcomed into and to have joined the bride's family
- how happy he is to have married such a beautiful, kind, and caring woman
- the appreciation he feels for his own upbringing and the good job his parents did

- some sort of response to the advice given by his new father-in-law

- an amusing story about meeting his bride or something that happened while they were courting

- thanks to the guests for their attendance (again, especially if they have traveled to get there,) for their kind wishes, and for the generous gifts

- a word of thanks and an expression of love and friendship for the best man, plus thanks to the ushers and anyone else who helped a great deal

- acknowledgment of the beautiful bridesmaids and appreciation for their participation; an expression of how much their attendance means to the bride

- a toast to "the bridesmaids whose beauty almost equals that of my wife," or just to "the beauty and elegance of the bridesmaids"

The Best Man

The responsibility of the best man is to respond on behalf of the bridesmaids. The luxury he enjoys, knowing that most of the serious thanks have already been offered, is the opportunity to entertain the guests with a few jokes and/or witty stories. Of course, this may come as a much more daunting prospect than simply thanking people but, alas, such is the plight of the best man. He might want to talk to the groom about that. He might want to express:

- the appreciation of the bridesmaids for the toast and for gifts given

- whatever comments or compliments he has for the bridesmaids

- his admiration for the bride, and the groom's good luck in having landed such a woman

- congratulations to the bride and groom

- what an honor it is to have been asked to be the best man

- a toast "to the future of the bride and groom"

- appreciation to the host and hostess (the parents of the bride)

- a toast to friends who could not attend

- the sentiments of anyone who sent a message to the bride and groom

- an agenda for the remainder of the reception

Preparation

The first question you may want to ask yourself before speaking at a wedding is, "Exactly what is my role here?" Were you asked to speak because you are related to the newlyweds and are hosting the event, because you tell great jokes, or because you have the benefit of years of wisdom and can offer wonderful advice to the young couple? How you answer this question could very well determine what your comments will be.

Planning Your Speech

Unless public speaking is something with which you have a great deal of experience and feel comfortable, it would be unwise to leave planning your speech until the last minute. Be comfortable with what you will say at least several days before the actual event, which, for those who lack experience, requires having done your research and put your thoughts on paper at least a couple of weeks in advance. Do not leave this until the last minute! You will only exacerbate your own anxiety!

Length

The well-seasoned and self-assured speaker knows exactly when he or she is straining the attention span of an audience. This person then cuts his comments short and exits while the guests are still amused and entertained. If you will be too involved in your own performance to get a good feel for the crowd, then plan on about five minutes for your speech. If the occasion is very formal, this may necessitate a bit more length, and an informal event is very flexible, in keeping with the mood of the wedding.

Research

As a general rule, there is a great deal less to be nervous about if you are fully prepared to speak. This requires knowing exactly what you are going to say, which in turn requires a little research. Relax. Nobody is asking you to hit the law library and find out what the principles of the Constitution were founded on. Begin by simply writing down a little information and deciding generally what you think you might say. Determine exactly where in your speech information is lacking, and then fill in those holes.

Is there a theme you want to stick with in speaking?
Of course, the concept of marriage itself is popular at
weddings. It is also something about which there is a
great deal of information. Would you like to personal-
ize your comments for the bride and groom? You
could ask either or both of their parents about their
weddings. What did they wear? Did it take place
during wartime? How many people attended? Who
performed the ceremony? Grandparents, aunts, and
uncles may also have stories to tell about weddings,
both theirs and someone else's. Intriguing information
can be divined by doing a little research into the
family history.

Composing & Editing
After you have made some notes and chosen a theme
or focus, take the time to eliminate unnecessary or
inappropriate information. Make certain you have not
inadvertently omitted anything that is essential to
your toast. There are five basic elements which, if
included in your speech, cannot help but improve it
a great deal, even if this speech will be your first.

STRUCTURE—what you want to say and the order in which you want to say it

SIMPLICITY—avoid complex ideas and unfamiliar words

CLARITY—express ideas as simply as you can

RELEVANCE—be certain to address your audience and the subject matter they are expecting

HUMOR—use only that which is appropriate, and best if it is from personal memories

Choose your words carefully. Omit anything that is tasteless, or that which may offend anyone in the audience. Remember, the focus of your comments should not be you, if done correctly.

Take the time to read your speech aloud in front of the mirror and then practice it on a friend or family member. Just having said the words a few times before someone who has to listen will help you when it comes time to do the real thing.

Reevaluate the speech after sharing it with someone.
Take out parts that do not flow or jokes that are not
humorous. Be prepared for any eventuality while you
are speaking. Whose to say someone will not pass
out in the punch bowl during your funniest joke,
thereby moving the spotlight quickly away from you.
It's okay! Remain composed and act as though you
thought it was as funny as everyone else, even if you
didn't!

Using Quotes
The Little Giant Encyclopedia of Wedding Toasts is
designed to provide you with a wealth of ideas and
humorous sayings which you can tailor to your
specific needs. For many, a mix-and-match approach
works well—this allows you to pull from various
themes.

Adapting Quotations
The more you can relate your quotations to your
audience and the people you are praising in your
speech, the more interested and flattered they will
feel. If the only quotation you can find is not very
relevant or complimentary, adapt it.

A Few Final Words

You may have noticed that the comments to this point have been geared to the traditional wedding. This is simply because most information on weddings is tailored to a traditional event. As you may have also noticed, the traditional wedding is arguably a male-oriented proceeding—the father of the bride speaks for his wife, the groom speaks for the bride, the best man speaks for the bridesmaids.

These are, however, no longer times in which women take a passive role. However traditional it may be for males to dominate the giving of speeches and making of toasts, it is certainly no longer the accepted norm. Keep in mind that weddings in the new millennium will certainly take on every shape and size, and who gives what speech and/or toast is no longer a matter of who is wearing the pants! Women speak for themselves these days, and weddings will forever be occasions in which uniqueness should be a treasured gift! Have a great day!

Toasts

When giving a toast:

❧ Be certain that all the guests have a drink in their hands, be it alcoholic or otherwise

❧ Make the toast positive and joyful, especially when using humor in the toast

❧ Name the person or persons you are toasting

❧ An example of an effective toast is: "Here's to the perfect couple, a better friendship and a stronger marriage never shall I see—to (groom) and (bride)."

To Bridal Couple

❧

May your hearts beat as one
from this day forward.

❧

To (bride) and (groom),
a case of love pure and simple.
(Bride) is pure and (groom) is simple.

❧

Here's to the happy couple,
may you grow old on one pillow.

ટ**

On a cold winter's day two porcupines huddled
together to stay warm. Feeling one another's quills
they moved apart. When the need for warmth
brought them together, their quills drove them apart.
They were driven back and forth at the mercy of
their discomforts until they found a distance from
one another that provided both a maximum of
comfort and a minimum of pain.
May your need for warmth be satisfied and
may you be spared the stab of your lover's quills.

ટ**

Ladies and gentlemen,
please stand with me as we raise our glasses in a
toast to the bride and groom, (bride) and (groom),
we wish you a lifetime of health and happiness.

ટ**

I feel honored to have been asked to give
the traditional toast to the bride and groom
on this momentous occasion:
(bride) and (groom), may your lives be filled with
joy, good health, and a lifetime of happiness.

❧

(Bride) and (groom), I toast you. May your joys be
many and your troubles be few, with only success
and good health following you.

❧

May all your days be as happy as the ones before.
(Bride) and (groom), I toast you.

❧

Please stand and join me in this traditional toast
to the bride and groom:
May the most you ever wish for
be the least you ever receive.

❧

Here's a toast to the lovely bride,
And to the husband by her side;
Here's to the home they're going to share;
May love and trust dwell with them there.

❧

May all of your ups and downs
be between the sheets!

❧

The most meaningful gift a father
can give his children is to love their mother.

❧

May you live as long as you want to,
and want to as long as you live.

❧

May this happy day
be the saddest of your lives.

❧

Here's to today.
Here's to tonight.
We shot the stork,
so it's alright.

❧

May we each be shelter to the other;
may we each be warmth to the other;
and may our days be good and long upon this earth.
— *inspired by an Apache Indian prayer*

❧

To (bride) and (groom),
may your love always be a factor.
I paid for this damn wedding
instead of buying my tractor.

❧

To the bride and groom—
may your coming anniversaries
be outnumbered only
by your joys and pleasures!

❧

Let us drink to the health of the bride,
let us drink to the health of the groom,
let us drink to the Parson who tied them
and to every guest in this room!

❧

Here's to the bride and groom.
May you have a lifetime of love
and an eternity of happiness.

❧

May all your troubles be little ones;
May all your troubles be small;
May all your troubles be light as air;
May you have no troubles at all.

❧

Here's to (bride) and (groom),
I wish you every success in your future
and every happiness in your marriage.

❧

Here's to the health of the happy pair,
may good luck meet them everywhere,
and may each day of wedded bliss
be always just as sweet as this.

❧

I toast you, (bride) and (groom),
as I wish you all the luck and happiness
in this world. May God bless your marriage,
and may you have a happy and contented home.

ॐ

Ladies and gentlemen,
it is now my pleasure to propose a toast
to the happy couple:
To love, which is nothing
unless it's divided by two.

ॐ

It is now my honor to toast the bride and groom.
To (bride) and (groom), two very nice people.
I wish you good health, happiness, and a wonderful
life together. Congratulations.

ॐ

It is an honor and pleasure to be asked to toast the
bride and groom. Please stand and join with me:
(bride) and (groom), we wish you long life;
Good health and a prosperous future.

ॐ

Here's to the husband—
and here's to the wife;
May they remain lovers for life.

❧

We all raise our glasses to you
as we toast your future.
May the joy and happiness of this day
remain with you throughout your married life.
God bless you both.

❧

(Bride) and (groom), I toast you:
May you always be as happy as you are today.

❧

It is an honor to be with you here today
to witness your marriage ceremony
and to share your joy.
(Groom) and (bride),
my heartiest congratulations,
and may all your troubles be little ones.

❧

Here's to health, peace and prosperity;
May the flower of love never be nipped
by the frost of disappointment.

ॐ

(Bride) and (groom),
congratulations on your wedding day,
and my sincere wishes go with you both.

ॐ

To the bride and groom—
may your wedding days be few
and your anniversaries many.

ॐ

Please stand with me as we toast
the bride and groom:
May your joys be as deep as the ocean
and your sorrows as light as its foam.

ॐ

Join me in a toast to our newlyweds:
May the happiest day of your past
be the saddest day of your future.

ॐ

May the road you now travel together
be filled with much love and success.

❧

I would like to propose this toast
to (bride) and (groom), wishing them joy and
happiness in their future together.

❧

Please join me as we propose a toast to the happy
couple: Our good wishes go with you for happiness
and a long and prosperous life.

❧

To the health of the bride and groom!
You will find that two cannot live as cheaply as one.
But, then, it is well worth the difference.

❧

To (bride) and (groom):
May this be one union that will never go on strike!

❧

I wish you health and I wish you wealth.
May fortune be kind to you,
and happiness be true to you
for as long as you both shall live.

❧

(Bride) and (groom),
may your love be as endless
as your wedding rings.

❧

May "for better or worse"
be far better than worse.

❧

A toast to love and laughter
and happily ever after.

❧

To a couple destined for a world of success,
not only in life, but in love.
Congratulations and good luck, my friends!

❧

May your marriage be touched by God's love,
a love that's as soft as the dawn,
as radiant as the sun,
as bright as the morning
and as beautiful as your wedding day.

🐝

The Divine brought you together
for a blessed reason.
May your marriage create
a permanent dwelling place for love.

🐝

As the two of you now become one
through this holy marriage in witness of God,
and all friends here,
may He bless you with Faith, Hope and Charity;
Faith—to believe in God,
Hope—to love and support each other,
Charity—to remember and love each person
that touches your lives.

🐝

May the Lord bless you and keep you;
May the Lord make his face shine upon you
and be gracious to you;
May the Lord lift up his countenance upon you
and give you peace.

❧

I wish both of you the patience of Job,
the wisdom of Solomon,
and the children of Israel.

❧

True love is a love that is timeless,
giving and growing.
It's a love that's shared between two hearts
through any circumstance of life—
through the hopes, through the fears,
through the joys and the tears.
What is true love?
It's love that needs no words to explain it,
but is demonstrated through
the hearts and lives of a man and woman.
It's the kind of love we see here today
between (bride) and (groom).
May your love be eternal.

❧

May you always look into each other's eyes
as you did the night you first met.

❧

To (bride) and (groom):
May God guide you, protect you
and keep you close to Him.

❧

Our God has created us a bride and bridegroom,
and because of Him, we rejoice.
May our marriage always be a testimony
to His love and providence.

— a Jewish toast

❧

Here's a toast to our bride and groom.
May your marriage life be filled with health,
wealth and blessings from your Higher Power.

❧

May your marriage be guided by the hand of God;
may your home be happy,
contented and filled with His Spirit;
and may He bless you every day of your lives.
To (bride) and (groom).

❧

May the bridge you began today
span a lifetime.

❧

As you make your way through life together, hold
fast to your dreams and each other's hands.

❧

To your wedding:
May your love for each other
grow as surely
as your waistlines will.

❧

To (groom),
the luckiest man on earth,
and to (bride),
the woman who made him that way.

❧

May you look back on the past with as much
pleasure as you look forward to your future.

❧

One and all, lift your glasses.
Here is to the bride and groom:
To your long health, to shared laughter,
to the magical and meaningful memories
you will create together.

❧

Here is to the twinkle of love in your eyes
that reminds each of us of our love renewed.
May God bless you and keep you.

❧

May you be blessed with the special joy
that comes from God above
and with the fruit of the Spirit, which is love.
To our happy couple.

❧

You see each other now
as the fulfillment of your dreams.
May you have the understanding
that today you begin your lives,
and there are dreams you have yet to share.

❧

May you share a joy that grows deeper,
a friendship that grows closer,
and a marriage that grows richer
through the years.

❧

May your joys
be as bright as morning
and your sorrows
but shadows in the sunlight of love.

❧

May your marriage
be wrapped in angel's wings
and all good things.

❧

May we all live to be present
at your Golden Wedding anniversary.

❧

May the garden of your life together
need very little weeding.

❦

May your lifetime together
be full and complete,
and your kisses together
be deep, warm, and sweet.

❦

May you both have
the patience to listen.

❦

Welcome to the next chapter in your life!
May your book of life
have a happy ending.

❦

May all your days be filled with sunshine,
all your nights with romance,
and all the time in between with love.

❦

May the twinkle in your eyes stay with you,
and the love in your hearts never fade.

It is said that the greatest happiness
is sharing one life
and one love forever.
Here's to the greatest happiness.

May all your children
have wealthy parents!

To the happy couple.
May your needs be few,
your blessings be many,
and your credit be limitless
and low-interest.

Here's to the groom
with the bride so fair;
Here's to the bride
with the groom so rare;
May every day
be happier than the last!

❧

May your good times be plenty,
your sad times be few;
May your love grow brighter with each day,
and with each day begin anew.

❧

To love is to learn,
and to learn is to forgive.
Best wishes to you both,
and may your love be long-lived.

❧

Live for the future,
learn from the past,
and enjoy the present.

❧

As you set out to write
a new chapter in your life
as husband and wife,
may you live a fairy tale romance.

❧

May you be blessed
with health, happiness,
and good harvest.

❧

(Bride), please put your hand on the table.
Now (groom), put your hand on top of (bride's)
hand. I want everyone in the room
to see the last time that
(groom) has the upper hand!

❧

May you be as one soul—
arms around one another
and eyes toward heaven.

❧

May you never lie, cheat, or drink.
But if you must lie, lie in each other's arms.
And if you must cheat, cheat death.
But if you must drink,
drink with all of us because we love you.

વ્ટ

May the sparkle in your eyes
light your path for the years to come.

વ્ટ

May the rest of your lives
be like a bed of roses...
without the thorns.

વ્ટ

Live each day
as if it's your last,
and each night
as if it was your first.

— *Shep Hyken*

વ્ટ

When you marry your best friend,
your lifesaver, your healer, your sweetheart,
you become whole.
To your love, falling softly on your hearts,
making you whole and complete.
You are compassionate, tender, caring people.
To your future!

❧

Don't look for the perfect spouse
in each other,
try to be the perfect spouse
for each other.

❧

Here's to the bride that is to be;
Here's to the groom she'll wed;
May all their troubles be light as bubbles
or the feathers that make up their bed!

❧

Here's to the bride and the bridegroom;
We'll ask their success in our prayers;
And through life's dark shadows and sunshine
that good luck may always be theirs.
— *Armenian toast*

❧

May thy life be long and happy,
thy cares and sorrows few;
And the many friends around thee
prove faithful, fond, and true.

❧

To our happy couple:
who has a marriage
made in heaven and lived on earth.

❧

To (groom) and (bride),
as they enter a sacred partnership,
the oldest partnership in the world,
the most intimate and the most enduring.

❧

Now you're married
we wish you joy.
First a girl
and then a boy.

❧

If necessary, sleep in separate rooms,
dine apart, take separate vacations,
have different friends.
Do everything possible
to keep your marriage together.

❧

May there always be such love between you,
that when one cries;
the other tastes salt.

❧

Congratulations on the termination of your isolation,
and may I express my appreciation of your
determination to end the desperation and frustration
that has caused you so much consternation in giving
you the inspiration to make this unification
and bring an accumulation to the population.
So as I end my toast to this occasion, and wrap up
my salutation, I raise my glass to this combination,
and bid good luck to the consummation!
So cheers, and on with the celebration!

❧

Here is to the groom who has never wandered. Here
he is in all his glory. Here is to the bride who knows
much better, but the groom's sticking to his story.

❧

When children find true love—parents find great joy.
To your love and our joy!

❧

May your marriage be like fine wine,
getting better and better with age.

❧

May the clouds in your life
form only a background for a lovely sunset.

❧

May your hands be forever clasped in friendship
and your hearts forever joined in love.

❧

May you be consistent in your decision
to love each other always.
And may you have this perfect,
total love forever.

❧

May Christ, the Light of the World,
shine at the heart of your marriage
and fill you with His joy!

To Bridal Couple (Contemporary)

To Fate that brought you together,
and to Love that will keep you happy forever.
Congratulations and God bless.

To precious moments of togetherness,
countless hours of sunshine and laughter,
days of indescribable joys and celebration.
May each morning be a happy surprise
as you awake in each other's arms
to discover that you love each other
even more than the day before.
To our newlyweds!

I wish you a lifetime of love,
a happy home and great success in all you do.
May you share equally in each other's love,
and may all your troubles be little ones.
Congratulations to our newlyweds!

(Bride) and (groom),
today is the start of something wonderful,
a brand-new life, a beautiful beginning.
Here's to a future filled with romance, delight,
sharing, laughter and great adventure
as your love grows with each day.
To your beautiful Beginning!

Thank you for letting us share in the joy
of this special day and for allowing us to bask
in the warmth of your love.
We wish you a hundred years of sunshine
and laughter, good fortune and good health
and, most of all, eternal devotion to each other.
Here's to (bride) and (groom).

I toast you, (bride) and (groom),
may the endless circles of your wedding bands
always be the symbols of your endless love.

❧

May your marriage have every season of happiness:
Summers filled with cloudless skies
and bubbling laughter;
Autumns filled with golden color
and encouraging smiles;
Winters filled with crystal beauty
and comforting hugs;
And springs filled with soft rains
and glorious new hope for the future.

❧

I would like to propose a toast to our lovely
couple—may the joy of your love grow deeper with
each hour, may your friendship grow closer each day,
and may your marriage grow richer
each and every year. I love you both. Cheers!

❧

Life is so much better when it's shared,
and I'm so glad you found each other.
May your marriage be bright and happy
because of the very special joys that come with
living...giving...caring.
Here's to (bride) and (groom).

કે.

Here's a toast to (bride) and (groom),
I believe love can last forever
and grow even stronger with time,
and that's what I'm wishing for you today.

કે.

May you always be there for each other,
partners in marriage as husband and wife,
may the sun shine brightly on your lives,
and may you always be as happy as you are today.

કે.

(Bride) and (groom),
may you enjoy the special moments of marriage,
when you stop to enjoy the little things,
those little pleasures so often taken for granted—
the lavender sunset, the fragrance after the rain,
the gentle caress and comforting touch.
Here's to a lifetime of sweet, precious memories.

કે.

I wish you joy of heart,
peace of mind
and the beautiful blessing of love.

☙

May your married life be full of the same joy
and happiness you feel at this moment.
May your love grow even stronger every day,
filling your future to overflow
with immeasurable joy.

☙

May the unbridled joy you feel today
be but a pale shadow of that which is to come.
Congratulations to you, and
God bless your marriage.

☙

I wish for you three things:
Warm moments shared together;
Thousands of tomorrows bright with love;
And a lifetime of dreams come true.
Cheers to the bride and groom!

☙

A toast to the happy couple:
to a long, beautiful married life together,
filled with peace, purpose, and prosperity.

❧

(Bride) and (groom),
we're really happy for you both,
and we wish you all the joy you deserve
from this day forward—the best is yet to come.

❧

May all your hopes and dreams come true,
and may the memory of this day
grow even dearer with each year.
To our newlyweds!

❧

Today your lives were joined as one.
From this day forward, may your burdens be lighter,
may your joys multiply tenfold,
and may your lives be doubly rich
because of the commitment you made today.
Here's to the beautiful couple.

❧

May you always share
the kind of love and joy you feel today.
(Bride) and (groom), here's to a beautiful life.

To the happy couple:
May your future be filled
with wine and roses.

To the happy couple:
May your future be filled
with wine and roses.

May every moment you share be sweet,
may every today you share be beautiful,
and may every tomorrow you share
be a glorious new beginning.
To (bride) and (groom).

(Bride) and (groom), my dear friends,
I speak from my heart when I say:
May you have the strength to change
those things that can be changed;
May you have the patience
to live with those things that cannot;
And may you have the wisdom
to know one from the other.
My prayers and best wishes go with you both!
— *inspired by the Serenity Prayer*

રતા

May your love be modern enough
to survive the times,
and old-fashioned enough
to last forever. God bless you!

રતા

I wish you a lifetime
of long walks and candlelight dinners.
To (bride) and (groom).

રતા

May this day always live in your hearts,
and may it be just the beginning
of your beautiful forever together.
Go with our love and Godspeed!

રતા

May your tomorrows be filled
with special memory-making times
yet to be shared—times
of gentle warmth and loving care.

May all your tomorrows
be promises come true.

Let us toast to the health of the bride;
Let us toast to the health of the groom;
Let us toast to the person that tied;
Let us toast to every guest in the room.

Here is to loving, to romance, to us.
May we travel together through time.
We alone count as none,
but together we're one,
For our partnership puts love to rhyme.

To the bride and groom:
May their troubles be little ones.

May the power of your love
bring you lasting happiness.

To the Bride

૨&

May she share everything with her husband,
including the housework.

૨&

Ladies and gentlemen, a toast;
to my best friend's new best friend.

૨&

Ladies and gentlemen,
please stand with me as we join
in the traditional toast to the bride:
health, happiness and all the best life has to offer.
To (bride).

૨&

Love, be true to her;
Life, be dear to her;
Health, stay close to her;
Joy, draw near to her;
Fortune, find what you can do for her,
search your treasure house through her,
follow her footsteps the wide world over,
and keep her husband always her lover.

❧

It has been my pleasure
to know (bride) all her life,
and no one is more delighted than I
to see her marry (groom).
Ladies and gentlemen,
please join with me
in a toast to the bride:
here's to your happiness,
today and always.

❧

(Bride), there was never a bride
more beautiful and radiant
than you are today.
Best wishes for a joyous married life,
full of good health and happiness.

❧

Let her remember that we gave her
this husband on approval.
He can be returned for credit or exchange,
but her love will not be refunded.

To the Groom

❧

To husbands:
Men when they are boys;
Boys when they are men;
And loveable always.

❧

He is leaving us for a better life.
But we are not leaving him.

❧

To that nervous, fidgety,
restless, impatient, uncomfortable
but enviable fellow,
the groom.

❧

A man usually spends
the better part of his life
searching for the right person.
In the meantime
he usually gets married.

A piece of cowboy advice:
"There's two theories to arguing with a woman.
Neither one works."

Here's to (groom)!
We always pegged him as someone
that would get one of those mail-order brides.
Tonight, he has done almost as well.

To the man who has conquered
the bride's heart, and her mother's.

Here's to the groom,
a man who keeps his head
though he loses his heart.

A toast to the groom—
and discretion to his bachelor friends.

❧

I've drank to your health in taverns.
I've drank to your health in my home.
I've drank to your health so many damn times,
I've almost ruined my own.

❧

Here's to the lasses we've loved, my lad.
Here's to the lips we've pressed.
Kisses and lasses,
like liquor in glasses,
the last is always the best.

❧

(Groom), now that you are a married man,
forget all your mistakes.
No sense two people
remembering the same thing.

❧

Remember (groom),
the key to a long and happy marriage
is to always say those three little words:
You're right dear!

❧

If we men married
the women we deserve
we should have
a very bad time of it.

— *Oscar Wilde*
(1854-1900) Irish poet/essayist

❧

Here's to the freedom
and pleasures of the single life...
May my memory now fail me!
— *Michael Macfarlane*

❧

Here's to man—
He is like a coal oil lamp;
He is not especially bright;
He is often turned down;
He generally smokes;
And he frequently goes out at night.

By Groom to Bride

❧

My greatest treasures are all our yesterdays,
but my greatest prize is our lifetime of tomorrows.
To all our tomorrows.

❧

This toast is to my beautiful wife.
(Bride), thank you for being so easy to love.
Here's to a lifetime of quiet moments
just for dreaming,
laughing moments
just for sharing,
and tender moments
warm with caring.
To my bride.

❧

I would like to propose a toast
to my best friend, my bride, (bride).
I'm so glad I married my best friend.
Because of our friendship, our marriage will be a
comfortable relationship where we feel understood
and accepted, always with each other's best interests
at heart. Here's to my wife.

❧

(Bride), you are joy to my heart
and food to my soul.
May our future be filled with laughter,
sunshine and our sweet, eternal love.
To my soul mate—
my wife, (bride).

❧

(Bride), did you know that no matter
how dark the day,
no matter how down my mood,
when you walk into the room,
the sun comes out?
To my sunshine—
the light of my life.

❧

To my beautiful bride, (bride).
May our lives be beautiful together;
May all our dreams come true,
and may I give back to you
the gifts of love you give me every day.

❧

(Bride), with this toast I offer you the gift of my
eternal love, given with a free and open heart.

❧

I would like to propose a toast to my wife.
From this moment forward I will share my life
with you as your husband,
and my love for you will never change
except to become deeper still as each day passes.
To my wife, (bride).

❧

(Bride), when I saw you in your wedding gown
for the first time as you walked down the aisle,
I wondered what I ever did to deserve such
happiness. I am humbled and grateful to have you
for my wife. My heart is full.
Here's to you, (bride).

❧

I would like to propose a toast to my wife, (bride).
With this toast I pass all my love
from my heart to yours.

ૐ

To your beautiful eyes;
They are windows to a beautiful soul.

ૐ

To the one I love:
May our lives together be blessed
with happiness and peace.

ૐ

When God created souls
and sent them into the world,
He knew all along that someday
ours would find each other.
To my eternal soulmate.

ૐ

To the most beautiful person in the world.
Thank you for sharing my life.

ૐ

I would like to propose a toast
to my bride.
Thank you for a chance to love
and to be loved.

❧

To you, my inspiration,
my light, my love.

❧

Because I love you truly,
because you love me, too,
my very greatest happiness
is sharing life with you.

❧

Here's to the girl
that's good and sweet;
Here's to the girl
that's true;
Here's to the girl
that rules my heart—
in other words,
here's to you.

❧

To my beloved wife—
we've only just begun.

❧

I would like to propose a toast
to my lovely bride, (bride).
I love you more than yesterday
and less than all our tomorrows.

❧

(Bride), we have only just begun
to see what our love can be...
to our unending future.

❧

To my wife, (bride).
I'm going to fall in love with you
all over again every day.

❧

(Bride),
you are my strength,
my treasure, my perfect one.
I thank God for bringing me
such a priceless gift.
To my wife.

❧

The greatest happiness—
the greatest gift possible—
is to be able to share my life with you.
Thank you for giving me this gift.
To my wife, (bride).

❧

To my wife, (bride).
You are a priceless treasure.
I will admire you, protect you, love you,
and hold you tenderly in may hands.
Thank you for choosing me to be your husband.

❧

A toast to my wife, (bride).
When we arrived here today,
we were two separate people.
But now we are united as husband and wife.
To one heart, one love, one life.

❧

Today, I married my best friend.
To my wife.

❧

(Bride), our time has finally come—
our wedding day—
our time to laugh,
our time to dance,
our time to love,
our time to embrace.
I thank God for bringing us together
in His perfect time.
To my precious wife, (bride).

❧

Because I love you truly,
because you love me, too,
my very greatest happiness
is sharing life with you.

❧

Here's to the prettiest;
Here's to the wittiest;
Here's to the truest of all who are true;
Here's to the neatest one;
Here's to the sweetest one;
Here's to them all in one—
Here's to you.

❧

To my wife,
My bride and joy.

❧

Here's to Eternity—
may we spend it in as good company
as this night finds us.

❧

Here's a toast for you and me:
And may we never disagree;
But, if we do, then to heck with you.
So here's a toast to me!

❧

I've known a lot of women,
and I've liked a few,
but I've loved only one —here's to you.

❧

Here's a toast to my bride, (bride),
and to a lifetime of loving
and serving each other,
just as our hearts long to love
and serve God.

❧

Here's to my mother-in-law's daughter;
Here's to her father-in-law's son;
And here's to the vows we've just taken,
and the life we've just begun.

❧

Here's to the night I met you.
If I hadn't met you, I wouldn't have let you.
Now that I've let you, I'm glad that I met you.
And I'll let you again, I bet you!

❧

Our dancing days have just begun.
To my beautiful bride, (bride),
may I have this dance
for the rest of my life?

❧

Here's to the girl I love,
and here's to the girl that loves me,
and here's to all those that
love her that I love,
and to those that love her
that love me.

By Bride to Groom

❧

Together forever
down life's long road,
through hills and mountains, valleys and seas,
we'll cross any obstacle, united we'll be,
the love we have is patient and kind,
a love that will last for all of time,
together now as husband and wife,
hand in hand, for the rest of our life.

❧

He knows all about me
and loves me still...
that's gotta mean something!

❧

I would like to propose a toast to (groom).
My dream was to find a man
who would understand me
without me uttering a single word,
a man whose values and spirit matched my own—
a soul mate. I finally found him.
To my soul mate, (groom).

❧

I would like to propose a toast
to my wonderful husband, (groom).
Today is our beautiful beginning
of a hundred years of happy tomorrows,
and it is a celebration of the very best
we have to offer each other.
Here's to you (groom)—
May all our dreams come true.

❧

For all the wonderful ways
you've touched my heart,
and for all the unexpected ways
you've changed my life,
I love you.
To my husband.

❧

(Groom),
you are my reason to run, to dance, to see,
to think, to live, but most of all,
you are my reason to love.
To my husband, (groom).
    — *Old Eskimo Indian wedding prayer*

To my husband, (groom).
May our marriage always
be a safe haven from the world
and a place of love and peace.

I would like to propose a very simple toast
to my wonderful husband:
Thank you for making me your wife.
I will always trust in your love
and you can always trust in mine.
To you, (groom).

To my husband and our shared future
filled with peace and happiness.

(Groom), today our dreams came true
as you and I became one.
Here's to our future
and a lifetime of new dreams
yet to come.
To my husband, (groom).

ઢ

To my husband, (groom).
May our marriage always be a testimony
of our deep and abiding love for each other
and for our Heavenly Father.

ઢ

(Groom),
with this toast may God,
who is the best maker of a marriage,
combine our hearts into one.

ઢ

To my husband, (groom).
May God bless our marriage
and make us pleasing to Him every day.

ઢ

May our marriage be protected by God's love.

ઢ

May our home be a safe haven filled with God's love;
may our marriage be a testimony of God's grace and
blessing; and may our future always be as bright and
beautiful as our wedding day.

By Groom to Bridesmaids

To the happy bridesmaids,
who today proved the truth
of Tennyson's sonnet—
"A happy bridesmaid
makes a happy bride."

(Bride) and I would like to propose a toast
to the bridesmaids.
How beautiful!
We appreciate your willingness
to participate in our wedding
and everything you've done
to help prepare for this day.
We can't thank you enough.
Please join me in a toast
to the bridesmaids.

Thank you for adding to the beauty
of this special day.
To the beautiful bridesmaids.

By Best Man

The worst thing
about being the best man
is that you don't get to prove it!

May the happiness
within your hearts today
be a mere foretaste
of the joys you'll experience
in the years ahead.
May all your dreams come true.
Here's to (bride) and (groom).

(Groom), I've never seen you happier
than you are today,
and it's all because of this wonderful woman
sitting by your side.
(Bride), thank you for making my friend so happy.
Please raise your glasses
and join me in a toast
to a lifetime of happiness for (bride) and (groom).

❧

As I stand here to honor our newlyweds,
I think of these words
written many years ago
by an unknown author:
"Time flies,
suns rise
and shadows fall.
Let time go by.
Love is forever over all."
My wish for you, (bride) and (groom),
is that your love will be forever over all,
always abiding over the circumstances
you will face as a married couple.
To your forever-type love.

❧

My wish is that your marriage
will be a thing of beauty
and a joy forever,
always as beautiful as you are today, (bride).
And may the loveliness of your marriage
increase with each year.
Here's to the bride and groom.

By Father to Bride

❧

Where are you going,
my little one, little one?
Where are you going,
my baby, my own?
Turn around and you're two,
turn around and you're four,
turn around and you're a young girl
going out of my door.

— *Malvina Reynolds*

❧

We fain would keep thee here,
yet there for thee they wait;
wife, daughter, angel, child,—
assume thy two fold state;

Leave a regret for us,
take them a hope the while;
Not without tears go forth,
but with a smile!

— *Samuel Longfellow*

they looked;
they loved;
'v sighed;

reason;
.ason
remedy.
— *William Shakespeare*
(1564-1616) English writer

what a delight you have been
to your mother and me.
and every stage of your growing-up years
brought us special joy.
You've given us so much happiness,
and today we want you to know
how very much you're loved.
It's time for you to leave your Mom and Dad now
and take this fella by the hand
and live with him for the rest of your life.
We hope and pray you'll be as happy
as you have made us.
Here's to (bride) and (groom).

🐌

Honey, you're "Daddy's Littl
You know that, don't you
You always have been and you alwa
even though you're a married woman
you've left our home to live forever with
You and (groom) will start a family of your
someday I'll be a grandpa to your own little
at least I hope that will happen,
but even then, you'll still be my little girl.
It's hard to let go—I'm sure you know that—
we've always been so close.
But, go with my blessing,
go happy and God bless you both.

🐌

(Bride), do you remember when you were little
and I used to read you a bedtime story every night?
You always loved the fairy tales
about princesses and knights in shining armor.
Well, Honey, today you're
a beautiful princess yourself,
and you've married your knight in shining armor.
Here's to (bride) and (groom) and their
" happily ever after."

&

(Bride), I'll never forget the day you were born.
I was filled with joy and wonder as I looked down
into your precious little face.
It was the first day of our life together—
you and your mother and I—
full of hopes, dreams,
and possibilities for your future.
Today is another special day—
a day that marks the start of your new life
together with (groom).
May your future be as bright with hope
as the day you came into our lives.
To the beautiful bride, my daughter, (bride).

&

All the years (bride) was growing up, we knew that
someday this day would come—her wedding day.
This is a very special day for us,
as well as for (bride) and (groom),
because it's a dream come true.
You see, (bride), it means so much to us to know
you've found the right guy and to see you so happy.
Go with our blessing,
and may all your dreams come true.

By Father of the Bride

I would like to propose a toast
to our new son-in-law.
You know it is said that
to lose a daughter
is to gain a son,
and we're proud to have you
as part of our family.
I might mention that in our case,
not only have we gained a son,
but a telephone!
Her phone bills will be
coming to your house now—praise God!
But seriously, as her parents,
we think your decision
to marry our daughter
was the best decision
you'll ever make in your life.
Here's to you, (groom).

❧

(Bride) and (groom),
Mom and I wish you every joy
and all our love as you set out together
as husband and wife.
If you ever need us for anything, anytime,
anywhere—you know we'll be there for you.
Congratulations to both of you.

❧

(Groom), welcome to our family.
We've already grown to love you as our own son,
and we wish you and (bride) a joyous future
as you begin your lives as husband and wife.
Here's to my new son.

❧

To see her is to love her,
and love but her forever,
for nature made her what she is,
and ne'er made another!

— *Robert Burns*

(1759-1796) Scottish poet

By Father of the Groom

It has been said that
when children find true love,
parents find true joy.
(Bride) and (groom),
you have certainly found true love,
that kind of lasting love that makes a marriage a joy,
the kind of love (groom's mother) and I
have had for more than ___ years.
Here's to our son and his beautiful new wife.

Our family has always been a circle
of strength and love,
and with every birth and every union,
the circle grows.
Every joy shared adds even more love
and makes our circle stronger.
Thank you, (bride) for joining our circle.
We welcome you with open arms and,
even though we've only known you for a short time,
we have already grown to love you.
We are so happy for both of you.
Here's to (bride) and (groom).

This is a pretty emotional day
for (groom's mother) and me
because (groom) has finally taken himself a wife,
and nothing could make us happier.
When children marry,
parents feel a blend of joy and sorrow—
the door that closed yesterday
opens tomorrow
with fresh dreams and memories
to fill our hearts.
We're overjoyed to have you
as part of our family, (bride).
God bless you both as you begin
your new lives together as husband and wife.

I would like to propose a toast
to our new bride and groom.
(Bride) and (groom),
thank you for the joy you have brought us
by the joining of your hearts
and lives together this day.

To Bride's Parents

❧

I would like to take this opportunity
to thank (bride's mother) and (bride's father).
You have been charming, gracious hosts
and it is an honor to be related to you
through the marriage of our children.
I hope our friendship continues to grow
through the years, and I know it will.
Here's to (bride's mother) and (bride's father).

❧

I would like to propose a toast
to (bride's) Mom and Dad.
You have raised quite a daughter here.
Thank you for entrusting her to me—
I will do my best not to disappoint you.
Thank you for accepting me into the family
as your son and for providing us with such a
memorable wedding day.
We love you!
To (bride's mother)
and (bride's father).

It's my wedding day,
a perfect time to tell you
how important you are to me
and to thank you for all you've given me:
a sense of the joy life can hold,
the ability to forgive
and the capacity to love
and be loved.
As I leave here today as (groom's) wife,
I'll take these gifts with me,
but I'll never forget
that I am your daughter.
I love you.

To my parents—
Thank you for sharing your love with me
Now as I begin my life with (groom),
I pray our new life will be filled
with the love you have had
for each other
throughout my childhood.
I love you both.

Bachelor Party

Here's to women—the bitter half of man.

Here's to the bachelor, so lonely and gay;
It's not his fault, he was born that way.
And here's to the spinster, so lonely and good;
It's not her fault—she's done what she could.

May all single men be married
and may all married men be happy.

May your union be like a game of poker:
Start as a pair
and end with a full house.

I wish you health;
I wish you wealth;
I wish you gold in store;
I wish you heaven when you die;
What could I wish you more?

Here's to keeping your bride
as close as you keep your wallet.

May we kiss those we please,
and please those we kiss.

To a beautiful bride,
a good job,
and good friends to keep you
from blowing it all.

May your new life
be hot enough to help you
forget your old life.

Here's to the girls—
the young ones,
but not too young,
for the good die young,
and who wants a dead one.

Friendship

❦

Here's to you, my friend,
and to friendship;
For the only way to have a friend
is to be one.

❦

Though both friends and wine you value,
as you've every right to do,
it's our wish, our dear old pal, you
keep the love and roses, too!

❦

May the hinges of friendship
never grow rusty.

❦

Here's a toast to the future,
a toast to the past,
and a toast to our friends, far and near.
May the future be pleasant;
The past, a bright dream;
May our friends remain faithful and dear.

❧

Here's to all of you, my friends.
I greet you.
And may I never cease
to greet you as "my friends."

❧

May our house always be too small
to hold all our friends.

— *Myrtle Reed*

❧

Here's to the fellow who makes us laugh,
who makes us forget our sorrow;
May he have a good, big bank account,
and friends who never borrow.

❧

May you live in bliss,
from sorrow away,
have plenty laid up for a rainy day;
And when you are ready to settle in life,
may you be a good husband,
and wed a good wife.

ₑ🍵

To our friends!
May fortune be as generous with them
as she has been with us in giving us such friends.

ₑ🍵

Here's to our absent friends—
although out of sight,
we recognize them with our glasses.
Let's drink!!

ₑ🍵

Here's to you, my friend—
may your soul be in glory long before
the devil knows you're dead.

ₑ🍵

Here's to my friend—
the one who knows I'm no good
and is able to forget it.

ₑ🍵

Here's to the tears of friendship.
May they crystallize as they fall
and be worn as jewels by those we love.

To our friends,
who know the worst about us
but refuse to believe it.

A health to you,
and wealth to you,
and the best that life can give to you.
May fortune still be kind to you,
and happiness be true to you,
and life be long and good to you,
is the toast of all your friends to you!

May we ever be able to serve a friend
and noble enough to conceal it.

To the lamp of true friendship.
May it burn brightest in our darkest hours
and never flicker in the winds of trial.

May friendship propose the toast,
and sincerity drink it.

Future

❧

May the best day we have seen
be worse than the worst that is to come.

❧

Here's to your future,
your present and your past;
May each new day
be happier than the last.

❧

To our life together.
As we walk the path of life,
always know my hand
is within your reach.

❧

As you build your home together
may you use the best
of what each of you bring to your union
and may you accept everything that is left.

Happiness/Joy

❧

I wish you all the joy you can wish.
— *William Shakespeare*
(1564-1616) English writer

❧

May you always be happy
in sunshine and strife,
as we have been happy as husband and wife.

❧

May we never envy those that are happy,
but strive to imitate them.

❧

May the sunshine of comfort
dispel the clouds of despair.

❧

Happiness is made to be shared.
— *French proverb*

ॐ

Here's to your health!
You make age curious, time furious,
and all of us envious!

ॐ

May our feast days be many
and our fast days be few.
— *Mary L. Booth*

ॐ

May you open your heart
and live long.

ॐ

May your heart be full of love always.
When the heart is at ease,
the body is healthy.

ॐ

A good life prevents wrinkles.
Here's to a wrinkle-free life together.

Home

❧

Here's to the home—
a man's kingdom,
a child's paradise,
and a woman's world.

❧

Here's to Home—
the place where you
are treated best
and grumble most.

❧

May the sunshine of hope
dispel the clouds of calamity.

❧

Here's to all our relatives—
may they forget our faults
and mend their own!

❧

May your love be everlasting,
and your home be filled with patience,
acceptance, and surpassed expectations.

Husband/Wife

દે🙵

To the model husband—
always some other woman's!

દે🙵

May you live in bliss,
from sorrow away,
have plenty laid up
for a rainy day;
And when you are ready
to settle in life,
may you be a good husband,
and wed a good wife.

દે🙵

You have been so supportive
of my search for myself.
What I have discovered along the way
is that I love you.
To you—and now—to us.

Love

&

I have known many,
liked a few,
loved one—
here's to you!

&

To the wings of love
that will let you soar even higher together
through the peaks and valleys life provides.

&

May our love be as strong as the willow,
and as willing to bend.

&

Here's to Love—
the only fire against which
there is no insurance.

&

Since love departs at dawn, create,
O God, a night that has no morn.

Marriage

੨੨

Here's to the bride
and mother-in-law;
Here's to the groom
and father-in-law;
Here's to sister
and brother-in-law;
Here's to friends
and friends-in-law;
May none of them need
an attorney-at-law.

੨੨

May those who enter the rosy paths of matrimony
never meet with thorns.

੨੨

Here's to marriage—
a ceremony in which rings
are put on the finger of the lady
and through the nose of the gentleman.
— *Herbert Spencer*
(1820-1903) English philosopher

❧

Here's to marriage—
that happy estate that resembles a pair of scissors,
so joined that they cannot be separated,
often moving in opposite directions,
yet punishing anyone
that comes between them.

❧

To a happy marriage:
the only sport
in which the trapped animal
has to buy the license.

❧

Here's to marriage,
for man is not complete
until he is married...
and then he is finished!

Romance

❧

The sun sets and rises
in your eyes.
To us.

❧

You are my rose
and my candlelight.
Wherever you are
there is love.

❧

You have given me a home in your arms.
Since I met you, I have learned what it is to be
loved. God bless our lives together.

❧

To all the memories we have shared
and the new ones we are creating.

❧

With you I believe I can do anything.
To us and a life full of prosperity.

Second Marriage

&

To our wives and sweethearts.
May they never meet!

&

Here's to the triumph
of hope over experience.

&

I would like to propose a toast to our newlyweds.
This day is especially precious
because you are so blessed
to be given a second chance at happiness.
What a wonderful day
of renewed hope and joy.
It is a day of peace and contentment—
a sweet calm after a cold fearsome storm.
We are so glad you found each other,
and just remember the best is yet to come;
Here's to (bride) and (groom.)

Libation

❧

Here's to the happy launching
of the Courtship
on the Sea of Matrimony.
May the rocks
be confined to the cradle.

❧

May the roof above you never fall in,
and may you both never fall out.

❧

May they find peace of mind
comes to all who are kind;
May the rough times ahead
become triumphs in time;
May their children
be happy each day;
God bless this family
who started today.

❧

In good times and bad times,
in sickness and health,
may they know that riches
are not needed for wealth.
Have them face problems
they'll meet on their way;
God bless this couple
who marry today.

❧

There they stand hand in hand
and exchange wedding bands.
Today is the day of all their dreams and plans,
and all of their loved ones are here to say
God bless this couple who marry today.

❧

As you slide down the banister of life,
may the splinters never face the wrong way!

❧

Long life and happiness—
for your long life will be my happiness.

As they go, may they know
every love that will show
and as life gets shorter,
may their feelings grow;
Wherever they travel,
wherever they stay,
God bless this couple
who marry today.

Those who are one with drink
are one in life.
Bottoms up!

While you live,
drink!—
for once dead,
you never shall return.

Wedding Blessings

❧

May God be with you and bless you;
May you see your children's children;
May you be poor in misfortunes,
rich in blessings;
May you know nothing but happiness
from this day forward.

❧

AN IRISH WEDDING BLESSING
May love and laughter
light your days,
and warm your heart and home.
May good and faithful friends be yours,
wherever you may roam.
May peace and plenty
bless your world,
with joy that long endures.
May all life's passing seasons
bring the best to you and yours.

❧

May the road rise to meet you.
May the wind be always at your back.
May the sun shine warm upon your face,
the rains fall soft upon the fields.
May the light of friendship
guide your paths together.
May the laughter of children
grace the halls of your home.
May the joy of living for one another
trip a smile from your lips,
a twinkle from your eye.
And when eternity beckons,
at the end of a life heaped high with love,
may the good Lord embrace you
with the arms that have nurtured you
the whole length of your joy-filled days.
May the gracious God hold you both
in the palm of His hands.
And, today, may the Spirit of Love
find a dwelling place in your hearts. Amen.

Success

❧

To our success!
Without you,
it would all be meaningless.

❧

May you find the serenity of oneness.

❧

Nothing is nobler or more admirable
than when two people who see eye to eye live
together as husband and wife,
thereby confounding their enemies and delighting
their friends.

— *Homer*

(before 700 BC) Greek author
The Odessey

❧

Live today to the fullest!
Remember, it is the first day
of the rest of your life.

Quotes

Adversity

❧

When a man steals your wife, there is no better
revenge than to let him keep her.

— *Sacha Guitry*
(1885-1957) French dramatist/actor

❧

Sometimes I wonder if men and women
really suit each other.
Perhaps they should live next door
and just visit now and then.

— *Katharine Hepburn*
(1909-) American actress

❧

A stumble is not a fall.

— *Haitian proverb*

❧

A woman has got to love a bad man
once or twice in her life
to be thankful for a good one.

— *Mae West*
(1892-1980) American actress

Trouble is a part of your life,
and if you don't share it,
you don't give the person that loves you
enough chance to love you enough.
— *Dinah Shore*
(1917-) American entertainer

Let me not to the marriage of true minds
admit impediments. Love is not love
which alters when it alteration finds,
or bends with the remover to remove:
O, no! it is an ever-fixed mark,
That looks on tempests and is never shaken;
It is the star to every wandering bark,
whose worth's unknown,
although his height be taken.
Love's not Time's fool,
though rosy lips and cheeks
within his bending sickle's compass come;
Love alters not with his brief hours and weeks,
but bears it out, even to the edge of doom.
— *William Shakespeare*
(1564-1616) English writer

❧

Brave admiral, say but one good word:
What shall we do when hope is gone?
The words leapt like a leaping sword:
Sail on! Sail on! Sail on! and on!
— *Joaquin Miller*

❧

Sweet are the uses of adversity;
Which, like the toad, ugly and venomous,
wears yet a precious jewel in his head.
— *William Shakespeare*
(1564-1616) English writer

❧

Sorrows remembered sweeten present joy.
— *Robert Pollok*

❧

If a relationship is to evolve,
it must go through a series of endings.
— *Lisa Moriyama*

❧

Every tear has a smile behind it.
— *Iranian proverb*

❧

A wise man will make more opportunities
than he finds.
— *Sir Francis Bacon*
(1561-1626) English philosopher

❧

In the middle of difficulty lies opportunity.
— *Albert Einstein*
(1879-1955) American physicist

❧

Don't wait for your ship to come in.
Row out to meet it.

— *unknown*

❧

Challenges can be stepping stones
or stumbling blocks.
It's just a matter of how you view them.
— *unknown*

Bachelors

A person without a spouse
is like a vase without flowers.
— *Cape Verde Islander*

A man's friendships are, like his will,
invalidated by marriage—
but they are also no less invalidated
by the marriage of his friends.
— *Samuel Butler*
(1835-1902) English novelist

Bachelors should be heavily taxed.
It's not fair that some men
should be happier than others.
— *Oscar Wilde*
(1854-1900) Irish poet/essayist

If you are looking for a big opportunity,
seek out a big problem.
— *unknown*

Beauty

❧

A man must marry only a very pretty woman
in case he should ever want some other man
to take her off his hands.

— *Sacha Guitry*
(1885-1957) French dramatist/actor

❧

Many a man in love with a dimple
makes the mistake of marrying the whole girl.

— *Stephen Leacock*
(1869-1944) Canadian author

❧

The lover knows much more about absolute good
and universal beauty than any logician or theologian,
unless the latter, too, be lovers in disguise.

— *George Santayana*
(1865-1952) Spanish philosopher

❧

If you get simple beauty and naught else,
you get about the best thing God invents.

— *Robert Browning*
(1812-1889) English poet

વ

"Beauty," said the lady, who was a powerful fairy,
"come and receive the reward of your good choice.
You have preferred virtue to handsomeness
and wit and you deserve to find all these qualities
united in one single person.
You are going to become a great queen..."

Saying this the fairy waved her wand, and everyone
who was in the hall was transported to the prince's
kingdom. His subjects received him with joy, and he
married Beauty, who lived with him for a long time
in a state of happiness that was perfect because it
was based on virtue.
— *Madame Jeanne-Marie Le Prince de Beaumont*
(1711-1780) French novelist
Beauty and the Beast

વ

She was good as she was fair,
None, none on earth above her!
As pure in thought as angels are:
To know her was to love her.
— *Samuel Rogers*

A beauty is a woman you notice;
A charmer is one who notices you.
— *Adlai Stevenson*
(1900-) American politician

Like a prune, you are not getting any better looking,
but you are getting sweeter.
— *N. D. Stice*

An eight-sided beauty is coldhearted.
— *Japanese proverb*

Shall I compare thee to a summer's day!
Thou art more lovely and more temperate.
— *William Shakespeare*
(1564-1616) English writer

What is lovely never dies,
But passes into other loveliness.
— *Thomas Bailey Aldrich*
(1836-1907) American poet/writer

❧

A thing of beauty is a joy forever:
Its loveliness increases; it will never
Pass into nothingness.
— *John Keats*
(1795-1821) English poet

❧

Beauty is that Medusa's head
Which men go armed to seek and sever.
It is most deadly when most dead,
And dead will sting and stare forever.
— *Archibald MacLeish*
(1892-) American poet

❧

Beauty is Nature's coin, must not be hoarded,
But must be current, and the good thereof
Consists in mutual and partaken bliss...
— *John Milton*
(1608-1674) English Puritan poet

❧

As the lily among thorns,
so is my love among the daughters.
— *Song of Solomon*

She walks in beauty, like the night
Of cloudless climbs and starry skies;
And all that's best of dark and bright
Meet in her aspect and her eyes.
— *Lord Byron*
(1788-1824) English poet

Lord of the far horizons,
Give us the eyes to see
Over the verge of the sundown
The beauty that is to be.
— *Bliss Carman*

She is not fair to outward view
As many maidens be:
Her loveliness I never knew
Until she smiled on me.
— *David Hartley Coleridge*
(1796-1849) English poet

Beauty is in the eye of the beholder.
— *Margaret Wolfe Hungerford*
Milly Bawn 1878

❧

Beauty is a short-lived reign.

— *Socrates*
(469-399 BC) Greek philosopher

❧

"Beauty is truth, truth beauty," —that is all
Ye know on earth, and all ye need to know.

— *John Keats*
(1795-1821) English poet

❧

If ever any beauty I did see, which I desired
and got, 'twas but a dream of thee.

— *John Donne*
(1572-1631) English poet

❧

A heart in love with beauty never grows old.

- *Turkish proverb*

❧

I shall wrap you in white linen and lilacs...
and deliver you to a morning in May.

— *Michael Macfarlane*

❧

Love preserves beauty,
and the flesh of woman is fed with carcasses
as are bees with flowers.

- Anatole France

❧

Remember that the most beautiful things
in the world
are the most useless:
peacocks and lilies, for example.

— John Ruskin
(1819-1900) English art critic/essayist

❧

...her beauty made
The bright world dim, and everything beside
Seemed like the fleeting image of a shade.

— Percy Bysshe Shelley
(1792-1822) English poet

❧

What is beautiful is good
and who is good will soon also be beautiful.

— Sappho
(620-565 BC) Greek lyric poet

Beginnings

Everything in life that we really accept
undergoes a change.
So suffering must become love.
That is the mystery.
— *Katherine Mansfield*
(1888-1923) New Zealand short story writer

With each new day
I put away the past and
discover the new beginnings
I have been given.
— *Angela L. Wozniak*

This day awaits my full presence.
I will be the recipient of its gifts.
— *unknown*

When you love someone,
all your saved-up wishes start coming out.
— *Elizabeth Bowen*
(1899-) Angelo-Irish novelist

❧

There is wonder and joy awaiting me, each day.
The growth I experience
is just what is needed at this time.
I am a student, and the teacher will appear.

— *unknown*

❧

Love yourself first
and everything else falls into line.
You really have to love yourself
to get anything done in this world.

— *Lucille Ball*
American entertainer

❧

Every day offers me many opportunities to grow
in acceptance and thus blessings.
I can accept any condition today
and understand it as an opportunity
to take another step
toward serenity, eternal and whole.

— *unknown*

Communication

❧

Saying that men talk about baseball
in order to avoid talking about their feelings
is the same as
saying that women talk about their feelings
in order to avoid talking about baseball.

— *Deborah Tannen*
You Just Don't Understand

❧

Kind words can be short and easy to speak,
but their echoes are truly endless.

— *Mother Teresa*
(1910-1997) Yugoslavian Roman Catholic missionary

❧

A good time to keep your mouth shut
is when you're in deep water.

— *Sidney Goff*

❧

Oh, what lies there are in kisses!

— *Heinrich Heine*
(1797-1856) German Jewish poet

✌

Two may talk together
under the same roof
for many years, yet
never really meet;
and two others at first
speech are old friends.
— *Mary Catherwood*

✌

One thing talk can't accomplish...is communication.
This is because everybody's talking too much to pay
attention to what anyone else is saying.
— *P.J. O'Rourke*

✌

Silences make the real communications
between friends. Not the saying but the never
needing to say is what counts.
— *Margaret Lee Runbeck*

✌

Never go to bed angry.
Stay up and fight.
— *Phyllis Diller*
(1917-) American entertainer

Family

❧

Be tolerant of the human race.
Your whole family belongs to it —
and some of your spouse's family does too.
— *anonymous*

❧

Mother-in-law:
A woman who destroys
her son-in-law's peace of mind
by giving him a piece of hers.
— *anonymous*

❧

I married the first man I ever kissed.
When I tell this to my children
they just about throw up.
— *Barbara Bush*
American first lady, 1989

❧

A man can't get rich
if he takes proper care of his family.
— *Navajo saying*

All that I am, or hope to be,
I owe to my angel mother.
— *Abraham Lincoln*
(1809-1865) 16th American president

Love matches, so called,
have illusion for their father
and need for their mother.
— *Friedrich W. Nietzsche*
(1844-1900) German philosopher

Women's liberationists spread the word that...
the only peaceful family
is one in which either the wife is enslaved
or the husband is androgynous.
— *R. Emmett Tyell*

Children are your heritage,
like arrows in the hand of a mighty man.
Happy is the man who has his quiver full of them.
— *adapted from Psalm 127*

❧

A mother is a mother still,
The holiest thing alive.
— *Samuel Taylor Coleridge*
(1772-1834) English poet/critic

❧

Honolulu, it's got everything.
Sand for the children,
sun for the wife,
sharks for the wife's mother.

— *Ken Dodd*

❧

...may her bridegroom bring her to a house
Where all's accustomed, ceremonious;
For arrogance and hatred are the wares
Peddled in the thoroughfares.
How but in custom and in ceremony
Are innocence and beauty born?
Ceremony's a name for the rich horn,
And custom for the spreading laurel tree.
— *William Butler Yeats*
(1865-1939) Irish poet
A Prayer for my Daughter

May your wife be like a fruitful vine
growing by the side of your house,
and your children like olive plants
round about your table.
— *adapted from Psalm 128*

The apple does not fall far from the tree.
— *American proverb*

Everyone is the son of his own works.
— *Miguel de Cervantes*
(1547-1616) Spanish novelist/poet

The child is the father of the man.
— *William Wordsworth*
(1770-1850) English poet

When you grow old,
obey your children.
— *Japanese proverb*

❧

A family starts with a young man
falling in love with a girl.
No superior alternative has been found.
— *Sir Winston Churchill*
(1874-1965) English prime minister

❧

A man must first govern himself
ere he is fit to govern a family.
— *Sir Walter Raleigh*
(1552-1598) English writer

❧

All the average human being asks is
something he can call a home;
a family that is fed and warm;
and now and then a little happiness;
once in a while an extravagance.
— *Mother Jones*

❧

Family jokes, though rightly cursed by strangers,
are the bond that keeps most families alive.
— *Stella Benson*

❧

He that hath wife and children
has given hostages to fortune;
for they are impediments
to great enterprises,
either of virtue or mischief.
— *Sir Francis Bacon*
(1561-1626) English philosopher

❧

All happy families resemble one another;
every unhappy family is unhappy in its own way.
— *Count Leo Tolstoy*
(1828-1910) Russian novelist

❧

God gives us relatives;
thank God we can choose our friends.
— *Addison Mizner*

❧

Children yoke parents to the past,
present and future.
— *Japanese proverb*

෨

One never realizes how different
a husband and wife can be
until they begin to pack for a trip.
— *Erma Bombeck*
American humorist

෨

There's a time when you have to explain to your
children why they were born, and it's a marvelous
thing if you know the reason by then.
— *Hazel Scott*
(1920-) Trinidad-born American musician

෨

The greatest thing in family life
is to take a hint when a hint is intended—
and not to take a hint when a hint isn't intended.
— *Robert Frost*
(1874-1963) American poet

෨

Financial success comes second.
My greatest accomplishment is raising my children to
be caring, contributing members of the world.
— *Caroline Rose Hunt*

Friendship

❧

Give her two red roses, each with a note.
The first note says "For the woman I love"
and the second, "For my best friend."

— *anonymous*

❧

Business, you know, may bring money, but
friendship hardly ever does.

— *Jane Austen*
(1775-1817) English writer

❧

There are three great friends:
an old wife, an old dog, and ready money.

— *Benjamin Franklin*
(1706-1790) American scientist/statesman

❧

Against a foe I can myself defend—
But Heaven protect me from a blundering friend.

— *D'Arcy W. Thompson*

❧

Never above you. Never below you.
Always beside you.
— *Walter Winchell*
American journalist

❧

There are three sights which warm my heart and are
beautiful in the eyes of the Lord and of men:
concord among brothers,
friendship among neighbors,
and a man and wife who are inseparable.
—*Ben Sira*

❧

Elysium is as far as to
The very nearest room,
If in that room a friend awaits
Felicity or doom.
— *Emily Dickinson*
(1830–1886) American poet

❧

Love is only chatter,
Friends are all that matter.
— *Gelett Burgess*

🍃

Friend of my bosom, thou more than a brother,
Why wert thou not born in my father's dwelling?

— *Charles Lamb*
(1775-1834) English essayist

🍃

Those friends thou hast, and their adoption tried,
Grapple them to thy soul with hoops of steel.

— *William Shakespeare*
(1564-1616) English writer

🍃

As old wood is best to burn, old horse to ride,
old books to read, and old wine to drink, so are
old friends always most trusty to use.

— *Leonard Wright*

🍃

Friendship, peculiar boon of Heav'n,
The noble mind's delight and pride,
To men and angels only giv'n,
To all the lower world denied.

— *Samuel Johnson*
(1709-1784) English poet/essayist

ॐ

A faithful friend is the medicine of life.
— *Ecclesiastes*

ॐ

Some friends come and go
But you are the truest friend I know.
— *Elsa Maxwell*

ॐ

True friendship is seen through the heart
not through the eyes.
— *unknown*

ॐ

Give me one friend, just one,
who meets the needs of all my varying moods.
— *Esther M. Clark*

ॐ

Your friend is the man
who knows all about you,
and still likes you.
— *Elbert Hubbard*

❧

Good health to you and me,
sweet neighbor, mine.

— *unknown*

❧

If, instead of a gem, or even a flower,
we should cast the gift of a loving thought
into the heart of a friend,
that would be giving as the angels give.

— *George MacDonald*

❧

There is so much friendship in love,
and so much love in friendship,
that it would be futile to ask where friendship ends
and where love begins.

— *Elizabeth Selden*

❧

A good friend informs you ever so discreetly when
you have spinach stuck between your teeth.

— *Joseph Cohen*

In all my loving, dreaming, suffering,
My best reward is your glad welcome for me.

— *Olavo Bilac*
(1865-1918) Brazilian poet

I have you.
A lover and a friend.
You are everything I need.
You are the sun, the air I breathe.
Without you, life wouldn't be the same.
Please never go away.
And if you go,
then don't forget to take me with you.

— *Basia*

Friendship is never established
as an understood relation—
It is a miracle which requires
constant proofs.
It is an exercise of the purest imagination
and of the rarest faith.

— *Henry David Thoreau*
(1817-1862) American writer/philosopher

&

And in the sweetness of friendship
let there be laughter and sharing of pleasures.
For in the dew of little things
the heart finds its morning and is refreshed.

— *Kahlil Gibran*

(1883-1931) Lebanonese poet/philosopher

&

Man strives for glory, honor, fame,
That all the world may know his name.
Amasses wealth by brain and hand;
Becomes a power in the land.
But when he nears the end of life
And looks back o'er the years of strife,
he finds that happiness depends
On none of these, but love of friends.

— *anonymous*

&

If I had to choose between betraying my country
and betraying my friend,
I hope I should have the guts to betray my country.

— *E. M. Forster*

Two Cheers for Democracy

A friend is a gift you give yourself.
— *Robert Louis Stevenson*
(1850-1894) Scottish poet/novelist

In great friendship there can be no questions
of weak and strong, of poor and rich.
Equality is the basis, and friends are equal
because they choose to be so.
— *Elizabeth Selden*

A friend is a person with whom I may be sincere.
Before him, I may think aloud.
— *Ralph Waldo Emerson*
(1803-1882) American writer

Friendship, which is of its nature a delicate thing,
fastidious, slow to growth, is easily checked,
will hesitate, demur, recoil where love,
good old blustering love,
bowls ahead and blunders through every obstacle.
— *Colette*
(1873-1954) French novelist

ଽ**

A friend doesn't go on a diet because you are fat.
A friend never defends a husband who gets his wife
an electric skillet for her birthday.
A friend will tell you she saw your old boyfriend—
and he's a priest.

— *Erma Bombeck*
American humorist

ଽ**

Love is friendship that has caught fire.
It is quiet understanding, mutual confidence,
sharing and forgiving.
It is loyalty through good and bad times.
It settles for less than perfection
and makes allowances for human weaknesses.

— *unknown*

ଽ**

Friendship is unnecessary,
like philosophy, like art...
It has no survival value;
rather it is one of those things
that give value to survival.

— *C. S. Lewis*
(1898-) English author

❧

Flowers are lovely; love is flowerlike;
Friendship is a sheltering tree.
— *Samuel Taylor Coleridge*
(1772-1834) English poet/critic
Youth and Age

❧

I do then with my friends as I do with my books. I
would have them where I can find them, but I
seldom use them.
— *Ralph Waldo Emerson*
(1803-1882) American writer

❧

The wish to be friends comes quickly enough,
but perfect friendship takes time to form.
— *Aristotle*
(384-322 BC) Greek philosopher/scientist

❧

Never shall I forget the days I spent with you.
Continue to be my friend,
as you will always find me yours.
— *Ludwig van Beethoven*
(1770-1827) German composer

No man is useless while he has a friend.
— *Robert Louis Stevenson*
(1850-1894) Scottish poet/novelist

The primary condition of friendship is joy—
the delight in recognizing yourself in another
and finding in him the person you have,
consciously or unconsciously,
always been seeking;
at least, you know him to be there,
waiting for you somewhere,
even as you were waiting for him.
— *Elizabeth Selden*

The only way to have a friend is to be one.
— *Ralph Waldo Emerson*
(1803-1882) American writer

O how good it feels
The hand of an old friend.
— *Henry Wadsworth Longfellow*
(1807-1882) American poet

❧

A friend is a second self,
so that our consciousness of a friend's existence...
makes us more fully conscious of our own existence.
— *Aristotle*
(384-322 BC) Greek philosopher/scientist

❧

Love is blind;
friendship only closes its eyes.
— *American proverb*

❧

The difference between men friends and women
friends is that men do things together,
women tend just to be together.
— *Art Jahnke*

❧

A true friend is a pearl
[who] reads your deepest needs
And so spares you the shame
of giving your heart's hidden desires a name.
— *Jean de La Fontaine*
(1621-1695) French poet/writer of fables

A friend is someone who comes in
when the whole world has gone out.
— *Emilie Barnes*

To me, fair friends,
you never can be old.
— *William Shakespeare*
(1564-1616) English writer

Your friend is your needs answered.
He is your field which you sow with love
and reap with thanksgiving.
— *Kahlil Gibran*
(1883-1931) Lebanonese poet/philosopher

How shall I continue the love I have inspired?
How shall I preserve the heart I have won?
Be lovely still, be gentle still.
The soul needs friendship,
the heart needs love.
— *Ed Habib*

❧

Friends need not agree in everything
or go always together,
or have no comparable other friendships
of the same intimacy.
On the contrary,
in friendship union is more about ideal things:
and in that sense it is more ideal and less subject
to trouble than marriage is.
— *George Santayana*
(1865-1952) Spanish philosopher

❧

Life is to be fortified by many friendships.
To love and to be loved is
the greatest happiness of existence.
— *Sydney Smith*
(1771-1845) English author/clergyman

❧

That is the best—to laugh with someone
because you think the same things are funny.
— *Gloria Vanderbilt*
(1924-) American designer

Friend Proverbs

A friend to everybody
is a friend to nobody.

Better a friend's bite
than an enemy's caress.

Better an open enemy
than a false friend.

He is a good friend
that speaks well of us behind our backs.

In time of prosperity, friends will be plenty;
in time of adversity, not one amongst twenty.

It is good to have friends
both in heaven and hell.

One enemy is too many,
and a hundred friends too few.

One may mend a torn friendship
but it soon falls in tatters.

Select your friend with a silk-gloved hand
and hold him with an iron gauntlet.

The best mirror is an old friend.

Trust not a new friend
nor an old enemy.

Your friend lends,
and your enemy asks for payment.

Geniality

As long as there are negotiations
there is hope for good relations.
— *Norma B. Smith*

Love cannot be forced,
love cannot be coaxed and teased
It comes out of Heaven,
unasked and unsought.
— *Pearl S. Buck*
(1892-1973) American writer

Oh, the comfort—the inexpressible comfort
of feeling safe with a person.
— *Dinah Maria Mulock Craik*

Happiness and peace are found
when we are in harmony with ourselves,
with God, and with our fellowmen.
— *Barbara W. Winder*

They may forget what you said—
but they will never forget how you made them feel.
— *Carl W. Buehner*

Seek always to please each other,
but in doing so keep heaven in mind.
— *Frederika Bremer*

It isn't only important for each of us
to be of service to others,
but it is equally as important
to be gracious receivers,
to allow others the blessings
that come from serving.
— *Janeen Hullinger*

Few things are more pleasing to see
than a grateful heart wrapped up in a young person.
It's a pleasure to be with him;
it's a joy to do things for him!
— *Winnifred C. Jardine*

❧

The most beautiful discovery
true friends make is that
they can grow separately
without growing apart.
— *Elisabeth Foley*

❧

There is an enormous difference between love
and like. Usually we use the word "love"
when we really mean like. I think very few people
ever mean love, I think that like is a much
easier relationship. It is based on sense.
— *Katharine Hepburn*
(1909-) American actress

❧

Unless you can die when the dream is past—
Oh never call it love!
— *Dinah Maria Mulock Craik*

❧

Nothing is menial
where there is love.
— *Pearl S. Buck*
(1892-1973) American writer

Golden Age

&

You are never too young to fall in love
and never too old to wish you had.

— *Carrie Noble*

&

It's never too late to have a fling,
For Autumn is just as nice as Spring,
And it's never too late to fall in love.

— *Sandy Wilson*

&

Come, madam wife, sit by my side,
and let the world slip, we shall ne'er be younger.
This day is ours, as many more shall be.

— *William Shakespeare*

(1564-1616) English writer
Taming of the Shrew

&

The secret is to become wise
before you get old.

— *unknown*

❧

Companioned years have made them comprehend
The comradeship that lies beyond a kiss.
The young ask much of life—they ask but this,
To fare the road together to its end.
— *Roselle Mercier Montgomery*

❧

First you forget names,
then you forget faces,
then you forget to pull your zipper up,
then you forget to pull your zipper down.
— *Leo Rosenburg*

❧

One of the oldest human needs
is having someone to wonder where you are
when you don't come home at night.
— *Margaret Mead*
(1901–1978) American anthropologist

❧

In youth we learn;
in age we understand.
— *Marie Ebner-Eschenbach*
(1830–1916) Austrian writer

You're only young once,
and if you work it right,
once is enough.

— *Joe E. Lewis*

Time–our youth–
it nevers really goes, does it?
It is all held in our minds.

— *Helen Hooven Santmyer*
(1895–1986) American writer

So come along; I will show you every
nook and corner of my Paradise.

— *Anne Sullivan Macy*

We read in the evening and are silent for hours;
at moments I glance at him or he at me
with a pleasant smile ever with joy.
I am very happy—winning him
by my kindness and meekness.

— *Anna Dostoevsky*

છ

Wrinkles should merely indicate
where smiles have been.

— *Mark Twain*
(1834-1910) American novelist

છ

Age is something
that doesn't matter,
unless you are cheese.

— *Billie Burke*
(1885-1970) American actor

છ

Grow old along with me!
The best is yet to be,
The lasts of life,
for which the first was made:
Our times are in his hand
Who saith, "A whole I planned,
Youth shows but half; trust God:
see all, nor be afraid...!"

— *Robert Browning*
(1812-1889) English poet

It is not the end of joy
that makes old age so sad,
but the end of hope.
— *Jean Paul Richter*

Chains do not hold a marriage together.
It is threads, hundreds of tiny threads,
which sew people together through the years.
— *Simone Signoret*

The first half of life
consists of the capacity to enjoy
without the chance,
the last half consists of the chance
without the capacity.
— *Mark Twain*
(1834-1910) American novelist

The only reason I took up jogging was so that I
could hear heavy breathing again.
— *Erma Bombeck*
American humorist

Gratitude

Don't think of gray in your hair.
Think of the fun you had putting it there.
— *Anna Greenwood*

I am beginning to learn
that it is the sweet, simple things of life
which are the real ones after all.
— *Laura Ingalls Wilder*
American novelist

Let your hearts rejoice in gladness!
— *Mabel Jones Gabbott*

We'll drink a cup of kindness yet,
for the sake of old lang syne.
— *Robert Burns*
(1759-1796) Scottish poet

❧

Flowers to the fair!
To you these flowers I bring...
Flowers sweet, and gay, and delicate like you;
Emblems of innocence and beauty, too.
— *Anna Laetitia Aikin Barbauld*
(1743-1825) English children's author

❧

There is no surprise more magical
than the surprise of being loved:
it is God's finger on man's shoulder.
— *Charles Morgan*
(1894-1958) English novelist

❧

He enjoys much who is thankful for little.
A grateful mind is a great mind.
— *T. Secker*

❧

My heart leaps up when I behold
A rainbow in the sky.
— *William Wordsworth*
(1770-1850) English poet

Happiness

❧

Happy the man, and happy he alone,
He who can call today his own;
He who, secure within, can say,
Tomorrow do thy worst, for I have lived today.
— *John Dryden*
(1631-1700) English poet

❧

All happiness or unhappiness solely depends
upon the quality of the object to which we are
attached by love. Love for an object eternal
and infinite feeds the mind with joy alone,
a joy that is free from all sorrow.
— *Baruch Spinoza*
(1632-1677) Dutch philosopher

❧

Success is getting what you want.
Happiness is liking what you get.
— *unknown*

❧

Happiness is an inside job.
— *unknown*

Happiness is the only good,
reason the only torch,
justice the only worship,
humanity the only religion,
and love the only priest.

— *Robert Green Ingersoll*
(1833-1899) American lawyer/orator

O, how bitter a thing it is
to look into happiness
through another man's eyes.

— *William Shakespeare*
(1564-1616) English writer

...the greater part of
our happiness or misery
depends on our dispositions
and not on our circumstances.

— *Martha Washington*
(1731-1802) American first lady

❧

Your life and my life flow into each other
as wave flows into wave, and unless there is peace
and joy and freedom for you,there can be no real
peace or joy or freedom for me.
To see reality—not as we expect it to be but as it
is—is to see that unless we live for each other
and in and through each other,
we do not really live very satisfactorily;
that there can really be life only where there really is,
in just this sense, love.

— *Frederick Buechner*
The Magnificent Defeat

❧

The action is best
which procures the greatest happiness
for the greatest numbers.

— *Francis Hutcheson*
(1694-1746) Irish teacher/philosopher

❧

You have earned your happiness,
enjoy it.

— *unknown*

৵

Whatever woman may cast her lot with mine,
should any ever do so, it is my intention to do all in
my power to make her happy and contented;
and there is nothing I can imagine that would
make me more unhappy than to fail in the effort.

— *Abraham Lincoln*
(1809-1865) 16th American president

৵

One should not seek happiness,
but happy people.

— *Coco Chanel*
(1883-1971) French dress designer

৵

The supreme happiness of life
is the conviction that we are loved.

— *Victor Hugo*
(1802-1885) French romantic poet/novelist

৵

Joy comes, grief goes,
we know not how.

— *James Russell Lowell*
(1819-1892) American writer

ॐ

At Earth's great market
where Joy is trafficked in,
Buy while thy purse yet swells
with golden youth.

— *Alan Seeger*
(1888-1916) American poet

ॐ

The greatest determiner of human happiness
is whether or not we have someone to love
and confide in.

— *Dr. Joyce Brothers*
American psychologist

ॐ

Heaven give thee
many, many merry days.

— *William Shakespeare*
(1564-1616) English writer

ॐ

Let us be grateful to people who make us happy;
they are the charming gardeners
who make our souls blossom.

— *Marcel Proust*
(1871-1922) French novelist

❧

Happiness consists not in the multitude of friends but
in their worth and choice.
— *Ben Jonson*
(1573-1637) English dramatist/poet

❧

Happiness isn't something you experience
it's something you remember.
— *Oscar Levant*

❧

The most wasted of all days,
is one without laughter.
— *e. e. cummings*
(1894-1962) American poet

❧

Happiness is a perfume you cannot pour on others
without getting a few drops on yourself.
— *unknown*

❧

I shall come again;
I like myself when I'm near you.
— *Elizabeth Mauske*

❧

They who inspire it most are fortunate,
As I am now; but those who feel it most
Are happier still.
— *Percy Bysshe Shelley*
(1792-1822) English poet

❧

We are each of us in this world
an angel with only one wing.
In order to fly,
we must embrace each other.
— *Luciano de Crescenzo*

❧

Do not think you can make a girl lovely
if you do not make her happy.
— *John Ruskin*
(1819-1900) English art critic/essayist

❧

The thing that counts most
in the pursuit of happiness
is choosing the right traveling companion.
— *Adrian Anderson*

Happy will that house be
in which the relationships are formed
from character.
— *Ralph Waldo Emerson*
(1803–1882) American writer

Most people are about as happy as
they make up their minds to be.
— *Abraham Lincoln*
(1809–1865) 16th American president

Wherever I roam,
whatever realms I see,
My heart untraveled fondly turns to thee.
— *Oliver Goldsmith*
(1730–1774) Irish poet/novelist

If you enjoy good health,
you are rich.

— *unknown*

❧

Once upon a time,
on a day that looked like any other day,
someone like no one else came along and made life
into something that would never be the same.
— *unknown*

❧

We have shared each other's gladness
and wept each other's tears.
— *Charles Jeffreys*

❧

The happiness of life is made up of minute
fractions—the little soon forgotten charities of a kiss
or smile, a kind look, a heartfelt compliment,
and the countless infinite smiles
of pleasurable and genial feeling.
— *Samuel Taylor Coleridge*
(1772-1834) English poet/critic
The Friend

❧

A pleasure shared is a pleasure doubled.
— *John Kieran*

Heart

❧

Now join your hands,
and with your hands your hearts.
— *William Shakespeare*
(1564-1616) English writer

❧

Two souls with but a single thought,
Two hearts that beat as one.
— *Fredrich Halm*
Der Sohn der Wildness, 1842

❧

Tears may be dried up,
but the heart—never.
— *Marguerite de Volois*
(1553-1615) French princess/scholar

❧

God, the best maker of all marriage,
combine your hearts in one.
— *William Shakespeare*
(1564-1616) English writer

❧

Maid of Athens, ere we part
Give, oh, give me back my heart!
Or, since that has left my breast,
Keep it now and take the rest!

— *Lord Byron*
(1788-1824) English poet

❧

The Devil hath not, in all his quiver's choice,
An arrow for the heart like a sweet voice.

— *Lord Byron*
(1788-1824) English poet

❧

The heart of the fool is in his mouth,
but the mouth of the wise man is in his heart.

— *Benjamin Franklin*
(1706-1790) American scientist/statesman

❧

The head is always the dupe of the heart.

— *François, Duc de La Rochefoucauld*
(1613-1680) French writer

❧

Bid me to live, and I will live
Thy Protestant to be:
Or bid me love, and I will give
A loving heart to thee.
A heart as soft, a heart as kind
A heart as sound and free
As in the whole world thou canst find,
That heart I'll give to thee.
— *Robert Herrick*
(1591-1674) English poet

❧

A candle loses nothing of its light
by lighting another candle.
— *unknown*

❧

No truer word, save God's, was ever spoken,
Than that the largest heart is soonest broken.
— *Walter Savage Landor*
(1775-1864) English poet

❧

As he thinketh in his heart, so is he.
— *Proverb 23:7*

&

We shall light a candle of understanding
in our hearts which shall not be put out.
— *anonymous*

&

When I was one-and-twenty I heard a wise man say:
"Give crowns and pounds and guineas
But not your heart away."
— *Alfred Edward Housman*
(1859-1936) English poet/scholar

&

A part of you has grown in me.
And so you see, it's you and me
together forever and never apart,
maybe in distance, but never in heart.
— *unknown*

&

The best and most beautiful things in the world
cannot be seen or even touched.
They must be felt with the heart.
— *Helen Keller*
(1880-1968) blind/deaf American writer

There is a courtesy of the heart;
it is allied to love.
From it springs the purest courtesy
in the outward behavior.
— *Johann Wolfgang von Goethe*
(1749–1832) German poet/novelist

If the heart could only be
heard, its every emotion would
be a great hymn for you!
— *Vasilii Zhukovsky*

Always there remain portions of our hearts into
which no one is able to enter,
invite them as we may.
— *Mary Dixon Thayer*
(1896–) American writer

My heart shall be thy garden.
— *Alice Meynell*

I know not whether thou has been absent:
I lie down with thee, I rise up with thee,
In my dreams thou art with me.
If my eardrops tremble in my ears,
I know it is thou moving within my heart.
— *Aztec love song*

Since the heart is yours that once was my own,
Your pleasure is my pleasure, right by right.
— *Christina Rossetti*
(1830-1894) English poet

The most precious possession that ever comes to a
man in this world is a woman's heart.
— *Timothy Titcomb*

All the knowledge I possess everyone else can
acquire, but my heart is all my own.
— *Johann Wolfgang von Goethe*
(1749-1832) German poet/novelist

The heart likes to tell us what we want to hear.
— *Gotthold Ephraim Lessing*
(1729-1781) German critic/dramatist

Through love, through friendship,
a heart lives more than one life.
— *Anaïs Nin*
(1903-1977) American writer

The mind divides the world into a million pieces.
The heart makes it whole.
— *Stephen and Ondrea Levine*

It is only with the heart that one can see rightly;
what is essential is invisible to the eye.
— *Antoine de Saint-Exupéry*

In a full heart there is room for everything,
and in an empty heart there is room for nothing.
— *Antonio Porchia*

Where your treasure is
there will your heart be also.
— *Luke 12:34*

The heart has its reasons
which reason does not know.
— **Blaise Pascal**
(1623-1662) French religious philosopher

What stronger breastplate
than a heart untainted!
— **William Shakespeare**
(1564-1616) English writer

The heart that loves is forever young.
— *Greek proverb*

The world has little to bestow
where two fond hearts in equal love are joining.
— *Anna Laetitia Aikin Barbauld*
(1743-1825) English children's author

Home

So long as there are homes to which men turn
At close of day;
So long as there are homes where children are,
Where women stay—
If love and loyalty and faith be found
Across those sills—
A stricken nation can recover from
Its gravest ills.
— *Grace Noll Crowell*

Home is where warm, circling arms
go all the way around.
— *Caroline Eyring Miner*

Never forget the real difference
between men and women.
A man comes home from a trip
and tosses his dirty laundry.
A woman comes home from a trip
and does it.
— *Elaine Cannon*
American writer

Stay, stay at home, my heart and rest;
Home-keeping hearts are happiest,
For those that wander they know not where
Are full of trouble and full of care;
To stay at home is best.

Weary and homesick and distressed,
They wander east, they wander west,
And are baffled and beaten and blown about
By the winds of the wilderness of doubt;
To stay at home is best.

Then stay at home, my heart, and rest;
The bird is safest in its nest,
Over all that flutter their wings and fly
A hawk is hovering in the sky;
To stay at home is best.
— *Henry Wadsworth Longfellow*
(1807-1882) American poet

You can be pleased with nothing
when you are not pleased with yourself.
— *Lady Mary Wortley Montagu*

A man's home may be his castle on the outside,
but it is his nursery inside.
— *Barbara Melton*

Sweet is the smile of home;
the mutual look when hearts
are of each other sure.
— *John Keble*
(1792-1866) English poet/clergyman

To be happy at home is the ultimate result
of all ambition.
— *Samuel Johnson*
(1709-1784) English poet/essayist

A good laugh is sunshine in a house.
— *William Makepeace Thackeray*
(1811-1863) English novelist

A light heart lives long.
— *William Shakespeare*
(1564-1616) English writer

❧

It seems to me that a woman
usually chooses the man
who chooses her.

— *Emily Bennett*

❧

Home is the place where,
When you have to go there,
They have to take you in.

— *Robert Frost*
(1874-1963) American poet
The Death of the Hired Man

❧

God of mercy,
God of grace,
Be pleased to bless
This dwelling place.
May peace and kindly deeds
Be found;
May gratitude and love
Abound.

— *Norma Woodbridge*

Humor

❧

A little girl at the wedding afterwards
asked her mother why the bride changed her mind.
"What do you mean?" responded her mother.
"Well, she went down the aisle with one man,
and came back with another."

— *anonymous*

❧

Republican boys date Democratic girls.
They plan to marry Republican girls,
but feel they're entitled to a little fun first.

— *anonymous*

❧

The woman cries before wedding;
the man afterward.

— *unknown*

❧

You know the honeymoon is over when
the breathless sighs turn to gaping yawns.

— *unknown*

It doesn't really take that much
to get married these days:
two loving people, a commitment,
a handsome groom, a beautiful bride,
a bag of rice...and about $25,000.

— *unknown*

The honeymoon is the vacation a man takes
before beginning work under a new boss.

— *unknown*

The trouble with some women is that they get all
excited about nothing—and then marry him.

— *Cher*
American singer/actress

Honeymoon:
A short period of doting
between dating and debting.

— *Ray Bandy*

❧

Any intelligent woman who
reads the marriage contract,
and then goes into it,
deserves all the consequences.
— *Isadora Duncan*
American dancer

❧

Whenever I date a guy, I think,
is this the man I want my children
to spend their weekends with?
— *Rita Rudner*
American comedienne

❧

I'm the only man in the world whose marriage
license reads: "To whom it may concern."
— *Mickey Rooney*
(1920–) American actor

❧

I know nothing about sex,
because I was always married.
— *Zsa Zsa Gabor*
Hungarian actress

❧

By all means marry.
If you get a good wife
you will become happy,
and if you get a bad one
you will become a philosopher.

— *Socrates*

(469-399 BC) Greek philosopher

❧

Laugh
and the world laughs with you.
Snore
and you sleep alone.

— *Anthony Burgess*

❧

A girl must marry for love,
and keep on marrying until she finds it.

— *Zsa Zsa Gabor*

Hungarian actress

❧

One survey found that ten percent of Americans
thought Joan of Arc was Noah's wife....

— *Robert Boynton*

❧

I recently read that love
is entirely a matter of chemistry.
That must be why my wife
treats me like toxic waste.
— *David Bissonette*

❧

I feel like Zsa Zsa Gabor's sixth husband.
I know what I'm supposed to do,
but I don't know how to make it interesting.
— *Milton Berle*
when called to the microphone
at the 2nd Annual
Comedians Hall of Fame Inductions

❧

I date this girl for two years—
and then the nagging starts:
"I wanna know your name."
— *Mike Binder*

❧

Better to have loved a short man
than never to have loved a tall.
— *David Chambless*

❧

Most married couples,
even though they love each other very much
in theory, tend to view each other
in practice as large teeming flaw colonies,
the result being that
they get on each other's nerves
and regularly erupt into
vicious emotional shouting matches
over such issues as toaster settings.

— *Dave Barry*

❧

I never hated a man enough
to give him his diamonds back.

— *Zsa Zsa Gabor*
Hungarian actress

❧

If variety is the spice of life,
marriage is the big can of leftover Spam.

— *Johnny Carson*
American talk show host

I'd marry again if I found a man
who had 15 million
and would sign over half of it to me
before the marriage
and guarantee
he'd be dead within a year.
— **Bette Davis**
(1908-1989) American actress

I've been asked to say a couple of words
about my husband, Fang.
How about "short" and "cheap"?
— **Phyllis Diller**
(1917-) American entertainer

Love is a snowmobile racing across the tundra
and then suddenly it flips over,
pinning you underneath.
At night, the ice weasels come.
— **Matt Groening**
American humorist
Love is Hell

ॐ

Jake liked his women
the way he liked his kiwi fruit:
sweet yet tart, firm-fleshed
yet yielding to the touch,
and covered with short brown fuzzy hair.
— *Jonathan S. Haas*

ॐ

Harpo, she's a lovely person.
She deserves a good husband.
Marry her before she finds one.
— *Oscar Levant*
to Harpo Marx
upon meeting Harpo's fiancée

ॐ

I take my wife everywhere I go.
She always finds her way back.
— *Henny Youngman*
(1906-) comedian

❧

Epperson's law:
When a man says it's a silly, childish game,
it's probably something his wife can beat him at.

❧

Women: If they're not turning down your proposals
for marriage, they're accusing you of suspicious
behavior in the women's lingerie changing room.
— *character Cliff Clavin*
"Cheers," American television show

❧

Love is a perky elf dancing a merry little jig
and then suddenly he turns on you
with a miniature machine gun.
— *Matt Groening*
American humorist
Love is Hell

❧

We had a lot in common.
I loved him and he loved him.
— *Shelley Winters*
(1922-) American actress

I don't think I'll get married again.
I'll just find a woman I don't like
and give her a house.

— *Lewis Grizzard*

When yer in a funk, people in love
are a royal pain in the patookus.

— *Portnoy*
"Outland," comic strip
by Berkely Breathed

You can't buy love,
but you can pay heavily for it.

— *Henny Youngman*
(1906–) comedian

Laundry increases exponentially
in the number of children.

— *Miriam Robbins*

ॐ

Anybody who claims
that marriage is a fifty-fifty proposition
doesn't know the first thing
about women or fractions.

— *unknown*

ॐ

I told my wife that a husband is like a fine wine—
he gets better with age.
The next day she locked me in the cellar.

— *unknown*

ॐ

You have to walk carefully in the beginning of love;
the running across fields into your lover's arms
can only come later when you're sure
they won't laugh if you trip.

— *Jonathan Carroll*
Outside the Dog Museum

ॐ

Flies spread disease—
so keep yours zipped.

— *anonymous*

Jimmy Carter as President
is like Truman Capote marrying Dolly Parton.
The job is just too big for him.

— *Rich Little*
American comedian

Always get married in the morning.
That way, if it doesn't work out
you haven't wasted a whole day.

— *Mickey Rooney*
(1920-) American actor

Love is blind,
but marriage restores its sight.

— *Georg Christoph Lichtenberg*

When a girl marries,
she exchanges the attentions of many
for the inattention of one.

— *Helen Rowland*

Husband

❧

Being a husband is a whole time job.
— *Arnold Bennett*
(1867-1931) English novelist

❧

American women expect to find in their husbands
a perfection that English women only hope to find
in their butlers.
— *William Somerset Maugham*
(1874-) English writer

❧

The only thing worse than being a bachelor
is being a bachelor's son.
— *unknown*

❧

A husband is a guy who
tells you when you've got on too much lipstick and
helps you with your girdle when your hips stick.
— *Ogden Nash*
(1902-) American humorous poet

The best way to get husbands to do something
is to suggest that perhaps they are too old to do it.

— *Shirley MacLaine*
(1934-) American actress/dancer

All husbands are alike, but they have different faces
so you can tell them apart.

— *Ogden Nash*
(1902-) American humorous poet

The majority of husbands remind me of an orangutan
trying to play the violin.

— *Honoré de Balzac*
(1799-1850) French novelist

My husband's mind is like a Welsh railroad—
one track and dirty.

— *anonymous*

A husband's last words are always, "Okay, buy it."

— *Nathaniel Parker Willis*
(1806-1867) American journalist

જ્ટ

He's the most married man I ever saw.
— *Artemus Ward*
(1834-1867) American humorist

જ્ટ

Being a husband is like any other job;
it's much easier if you like your boss.
— *anonymous*

જ્ટ

If a husband has troubles,
he should tell his wife.
If he hasn't,
he should tell the world
how he does it.
— *Nathaniel Parker Willis*
(1806-1867) American journalist

જ્ટ

A husband is a man who,
two minutes after his head touches the pillow,
is snoring like an overloaded omnibus.
— *Ogden Nash*
(1902-) American humorous poet

❧

Husbands,
love your wives
as you love your own bodies.
In loving his wife a man loves himself.
For no one ever hated his own body:
on the contrary,
he provides and cares for it;
and thus it is that a man
shall leave his father and mother
and shall be joined to his wife
and the two shall become one flesh.
It is a great truth that is hidden here...
— *Ephesians 4:25-32*

❧

It is easier to be a lover
than a husband
for the simple reason that
it is more difficult to be witty every day
than to say pretty things from time to time.
— *Honoré de Balzac*
(1799-1850) French novelist
Physiologie du mariage, 1829

❧

An archaeologist is the best husband
a woman can have;
the older she gets,
the more interested he is in her.
— *Agatha Christie*
(1890–1976) English mystery writer

❧

A husband is what's left of the lover
after the nerve has been extracted.
— *Helen Rowland*

❧

Husbands never become good;
they merely become proficient.
— *Henry Louis Mencken*
(1880–1956) American editor

❧

Husband: a man who buys his football tickets
four months in advance
and waits until December 24
to do his Christmas shopping.
— *anonymous*

❧

Back of every achievement is a proud wife
and a surprised mother-in-law.

— *Brooks Hays*

❧

It can't be easy being the husband
of a modern woman.
She is everything his mother wasn't
and nothing she was.

— *Mabel Ulrich, M.D.*

❧

A grateful son, long happily married, told in one
short sentence what his father had said when he
confided in his father concerning his coming
marriage to a lovely girl. This his father said: "Be
good to her—and treat her like a queen."

— *Thomas S. Priday*

❧

Husbands are like fires.
They go out if unattended.

— *Zsa Zsa Gabor*
Hungarian actress

ख़

Marital Freedom:
The liberty that allows a husband
to do exactly that which his wife pleases.

— *anonymous*

ख़

The average husband is worth about
twice what his wife thinks of him
and half what his mother thinks of him.

— *unknown*

ख़

Husbands are awkward things to deal with;
even keeping them in hot water
will not make them tender.

— *Mary Buckley*

ख़

A lover may be a shadowy creature,
but husbands are made of flesh and blood.

— *Amy Levy*

Infidelity

❦

A Code of Honor:
Never approach a friend's girlfriend or wife
with mischief as your goal.
There are just too many women in the world
to justify that sort of dishonorable behavior.
Unless she's "really" attractive.
— *Bruce Jay Friedman*

❦

I'm an excellent housckeeper.
Every time I get a divorce,
I keep the house.
— *Zsa Zsa Gabor*
Hungarian actress

❦

Bigamy is one way of avoiding
the painful publicity of divorce
and the expense of alimony.
— *Oliver Herford*

When you're away, I'm restless, lonely
Wretched, bored, dejected; only
here's the rub, my darling dear,
I feel the same when you are here.
— *Samuel Hoffenstein*

There is nothing better for the spirit
or the body than a love affair.
It elevates the thoughts
and flattens the stomachs.
— *Barbara Howar*

Eighty percent of married men cheat in America.
The rest cheat in Europe.
— *Jackie Mason*
(1934-) comedian

I guess the only way to stop divorce
is to stop marriage.
— *Will Rogers*
(1879-1935) American humorist

Morality consists in suspecting other people
of not being legally married.
— *George Bernard Shaw*
(1856–1950) Irish dramatist

I think every woman is entitled to
a middle husband she can forget.
— *Adela Rogers St. John*

Marriage enables a husband to find out what kind of
husband his wife would have preferred.
— *anonymous*

It is as absurd to pretend
that one cannot love the same woman always,
as to pretend that a good artist
needs several violins
to execute a piece of music.
— *Honoré de Balzac*
(1799–1850) French novelist

Joy

Nothing happens unless first a dream.
— *Carl Sandburg*
(1878-1967) American poet

Joy is not in things;
it is in us.
— *Richard Wagner*
(1813-1883) German operatic composer

May your heart be as light and bright
as an angel's song.

— *anonymous*

Nothing ever becomes real till it is experienced.
— *John Keats*
(1795-1821) English poet

Joy is Love when it is shared.
— *Kathy Davis*

꒰

Today a new sun rises for me;
everything lives, everything is animated,
everything seems to speak to me of my passion,
everything invites me to cherish it.
— *Anne De Lenclos*

꒰

Joy is an elation of spirit—of a spirit which trusts in
the goodness and truth of its own possessions.
— *Lucius Annaeus Seneca*
(4 BC AD 65) Roman philosopher/author

꒰

Joy seems to me a step beyond happiness—
happiness is a sort of atmosphere you can live in
sometimes when you're lucky. Joy is a light that fills
you with hope and faith and love.
— *Adela Rogers St. Johns*

꒰

The worst sin—
perhaps the only sin—passion can commit,
is to be joyless.
— *Dorothy L. Sayers*
(1893 1957) English author

୧▲

You will find as you look back upon your life
that the moments when you have really lived
are the moments when you have done things
in the spirit of love.
— *Henry Drummond*

୧▲

Joy is a net of love
by which you can catch souls.
- *Mother Teresa*
(1910-1997) Yugoslavian Roman Catholic missionary

୧▲

There are three principal postures of love.
It gives with joy,
receives with appreciation
and rebukes with humility and hope.
— *Albert M. Wells, Jr.*

୧▲

I found more joy in sorrow,
Than you could find in joy.
— *Sara Teasdale*
(1884-1933) American poet

ॐ

Now is the time to rejoice in your triumphs,
revel in your strengths,
and appreciate how awe inspiring you are.

— *anonymous*

ॐ

Love puts the fun in together...
the sad in apart...the hope in tomorrow...
the joy in a heart.

— *unknown*

ॐ

I have drunk deep of joy,
And I will taste no other wine tonight.

— *Percy Bysshe Shelley*
(1792-1822) English poet

ॐ

The sea has its pearls,
The heaven its stars—
But my heart, my heart,
My heart has its love!

— *Heinrich Heine*
(1797-1856) German Jewish poet

❧

The sort of girl I liked to see
Smiles down from her great height at me.
— *John Betjeman*
(1906-1984) English poet

❧

Men without joy seem like corpses.
— *Käthe Kollwitz*
(1867-1945) German printmaker/sculptor

❧

Stretch out your hand and take the world's wide gift
of Joy and Beauty.
— *Corinne Roosevelt Robinson*

❧

Weeping may endure for a night,
but joy cometh in the morning.
— *Psalms 30:5*

❧

The pleasure of what we enjoy
is lost by coveting more.
— *Daniel Defoe*
(1660-1731) English journalist

Take joy home,
And make a place in thy great heart for her,
And give her time to grow,
and cherish her;
Then will she come, and oft will sing to thee,...
It is a comely fashion to be glad;
Joy is the grace we say to God.
— *Jean Ingelow*

The joy of life is variety; the tenderest love requires
to be rekindled by intervals of absence.
— *Samuel Johnson*
(1709-1784) English poet/essayist

And I will make thee beds of roses
And a thousand fragrant posies.
— *Christopher Marlowe*
(1564-1593) English poet/dramatist

It is by believing, hoping, loving, and doing
that man finds joy and peace.
— *John Lancaster Spalding*

Kindness

It destroys one's nerves to be amiable everyday to
the same human being.
— *Benjamin Disraeli*
(1804-1881) English statesman/author

Try praising your wife,
even if it does frighten her at first.
— *Billy Sunday*
(1862-1935) American evangelist

No act of kindness,
no matter how small,
is ever wasted.

— *Aesop*
(6th century BC) Greek author

Be ye kind to one another.
— *Ephesians 4:32*

❧

'Twas a thief said the last kind word to Christ:
Christ took the kindness, and forgave the theft.

— **Robert Browning**
(1812-1889) English poet

❧

If I can stop one heart from breaking,
I shall not live in vain;
If I can ease one life the aching,
Or cool one pain,
Or help one fainting robin,
Unto his nest again,
I shall not live in vain.

— **Emily Dickinson**
(1830-1886) American poet

❧

Let me be a little kinder,
Let me be a little blinder
To the faults of those around me.

— **Edgar A. Guest**
(1881-1959) American poet

❧

A compliment is like a kiss through a veil.
— *Victor Hugo*
(1802-1885) French romantic poet/novelist

❧

I love thee for a heart that's kind—
Not for the knowledge in thy mind.
— *William Henry Davies*
(1871-1940) Welsh poet

❧

Kindness in words creates confidence. Kindness in
thinking creates profoundness. Kindness in giving
creates love.
— *Lao-tzu*
(604-531 BC) Chinese philosopher

❧

God loveth a cheerful giver.
— *II Corinthians 9:7*

❧

We pardon to the extent that we love.
— *François, Duc de La Rochefoucauld*
(1613-1680) French writer

❧

Let me live in my house
by the side of the road
And be a friend to man.
— *Sam Walter Foss*

❧

The verb "to love" in Persian is "to have a friend."
"I love you" translated literally is
"I have you as a friend,"
and "I don't like you" simply means
"I don't have you as a friend."
— *Shusha Guppy*

❧

It is man's peculiar duty
to love even those who wrong him.
— *Marcus Aurelius*

❧

Give a little love to a child,
and you get a great deal back.
— *John Ruskin*
(1819–1900) English art critic/essayist

Libation

❧

Were't the last drop in the well,
An I gasp'd upon the brink,
Ere my fainting spirit fell,
'Tis to thee that I would drink.

— *Lord Byron*
(1788-1824) English poet

❧

Drink to me only with thine eyes,
And I will pledge with mine;
Or leave a kiss within the cup,
And I'll not look for wine.

— *Ben Jonson*
(1573-1637) English dramatist/poet

❧

The innkeeper loves the drunkard,
but not for a son-in-law.

— *Yiddish proverb*

❧

Bronze is the mirror of the form; wine, of the heart.

— *Aeschylus*
(525-456 BC) Athenian dramatist

First the man takes a drink.
then the drink takes a drink,
then the drink takes the man.

— *Japanese proverb*

Bacchus' blessings are a treasure
Drinking is the soldier's pleasure:
Rich the treasure, sweet the pleasure,
Sweet is pleasure after pain.

— *John Dryden*
(1631–1700) English poet

If all be true that I do think,
There are five reasons we should drink;
Good wine—a friend—or being dry—
Or lest we should be by and by—
Or any other reason why.

— *Henry Aldrich*

Candy is dandy, but liquor is quicker.

— *Ogden Nash*
(1902–) American humorous poet

❧

Come, landlord, fill the flowing bowl
until it does run over. Tonight we will all be merry—
tomorrow we'll get sober.
— *John Fletcher*
(1579-1625 English poet/playwright

❧

If I ever marry a wife,
I'll marry a landlord's daughter,
For then I may sit in the bar,
And drink cold brandy and water.
— *Charles Lamb*
(1775-1834) English essayist

❧

Drink! For you know not whence you came, nor why;
Drink! For you know not why your go, nor where.
— *Omar Khayyam*
(-1123) Persian poet

❧

In wine there is truth.
— *Pliny, the Elder*
(23-79 AD) Italian scholar historian

❧

And malt does more than Milton can
To justify God's ways to man.
— *Alfred Edward Housman*
(1859-1936) English poet/scholar

❧

God made man
Frail as a bubble;
God made Love,
Love made trouble.
God made the Vine,
Was it a sin
That man made Wine
To drown Trouble in?
— *Oliver Herford*

❧

O God, that men should put an enemy
in their mouths to steal away their brains!
That we should, with joy,
pleasance, revel and applause,
transform ourselves into beasts!
— *William Shakespeare*
(1564-1616) English writer

Love

❧

Love begins with a smile,
grows with a kiss,
and ends with a teardrop.

— *anonymous*

❧

We always believe our first love is our last,
and our last love our first.

— *anonymous*

❧

Art is beauty,
romance is art,
and love is always love.

— *Venus de Milo*

❧

Because of deep love,
one is courageous.

— *Lao-tzu*

(604-531 BC) Chinese philosopher

ॐ

Who walks a road with love
will never walk that road alone again.
— *Charles Thomas Davis*

ॐ

At the touch of love,
everyone becomes a poet.

— *Plato*
(429-347 BC) Greek philosopher

ॐ

I sighed as a lover,
I obeyed as a son.

—*Edward Gibbon*
(1737-1794) English historian

ॐ

We come to love
not by finding a perfect person,
but by learning to see
an imperfect person perfectly.

— *anonymous*

ह‍

It's love,
it's love that makes the world go 'round.
— *anonymous*

ह‍

Love comforteth
like sunshine after rain.
— **William Shakespeare**
(1564-1616) English writer

ह‍

Every moment we share further
increases my capacity for love.
— *Elizabeth Forsythe Hailey*

ह‍

Whatever you do...
love those who love you.
— *François-Marie Arouet de Voltaire*
(1694-1778) French philosophical writer

ह‍

My love for you is mixed throughout my body...
— *Love Songs of the New Kingdom*

જી

Love conquers all.

— *Virgil*
(70–19 BC) Roman poet

જી

And to his eye
There was but one beloved face on earth
And that was shining on him.

— *Lord Byron*
(1788–1824) English poet

જી

Love—is anterior to Life—
Posterior—to Death—
Initial of Creation, and
The Exponent of Earth.

— *Emily Dickinson*
(1830–1886) American poet

જી

'Tis better to have loved and lost
than never to have loved at all.

— *Lord Alfred Tennyson*
(1809–1892) English poet

And on her lover's arm she leant,
And round her waist she felt it fold,
And far across the hills they went
In the new world which is the old.
— *Lord Alfred Tennyson*
(1809-1892) English poet

The course of true love never did run smooth.
— *William Shakespeare*
(1564-1616) English writer

Love vanquishes time.
To lovers, a moment can be eternity,
eternity can be the tick of a clock.
Across the barriers of time and the ultimate destiny,
love persists, for the home of the beloved absent or
present, is always in the mind and heart.
Absence does not diminish love.
— *Mary Parrish*

ଏକ

Practice random beauty
and senseless acts of love.

— *anonymous*

ଏକ

In their first passion women love their lovers,
in the others they love love.
— *François, Duc de La Rochefoucauld*
(1613-1680) French writer

ଏକ

There is nothing like a dream to create the future.
— *Victor Hugo*
(1802-1885) French romantic poet/novelist

ଏକ

Love is not blind,
it sees more not less;
But because it sees more
it chooses to see less.

— *unknown*

❧

Learn to wait before giving all your love—
thus you will be spared the feeling of having been
cheated. But a man who loves you so much that he
will share all the suffering and all difficulties with
you, and for whom you can do the same—such a
man you may love, and believe me, the happiness
you will find with him will repay you for the waiting.

— *Rose Schösinger*

❧

I have for the first time
found what I can truly love—
I have found you.
You are my sympathy—
my better self—my good angel—
I am bound to you with a strong attachment.
I think you good, gifted, lovely:
a fervent, a solemn passion is conceived in my heart;
it leans to you,
draws you to my center and spring of life,
wraps my existence about you—and,
kindling in pure, powerful flame,
fuses you and me in one.

— *Charlotte Brontë*
(1816-1855) English writer

❧

Fast—anchor'd eternal O love!
O woman I love! O bride!
O wife! more resistless than I can tell,
the thought of you!
— *Walt Whitman*
(1819-1892) American poet

❧

Without you, dearest dearest,
I couldn't see or hear or feel
or think—or live—I love you so
and I'm never in all our lives
going to let us be apart another night.
— *Zelda Fitzgerald*

❧

I love you so much that without you
I'd have so much less than nothing
that it wouldn't bear thinking of.
Will you marry me,
and trust me to make something of my life?
— *Helen Hooven Santmyer*

Peace and love
are always alive in us,
but we are not always alive
to peace and love.
— *Julian of Norwich*

I wandered lost in yesterday,
wanting to fly,
but scared to try.
Then someone like you found someone like me.
And suddenly, nothing is the same.
— *Leslie Bricusse*

And when love speaks,
the voice of all the gods
makes heaven drowsy with the harmony.
— *William Shakespeare*
(1564-1616) English writer

Nobody dies from the lack of sex.
It's lack of love we die from.
— *Margaret Atwood*

&

I confess that I love him
I rejoice that I love him
I thank the maker of Heaven and Earth
that gave him me to love
the exultation floods me.

— *Emily Dickinson*
(1830-1886) American poet

&

You
Deep in the heart of me,
Nothing but You!
See through the art of me—
Deep in the heart of me
Find the best part of me,
Changeless and true.
Deep in the heart of me
Nothing but You!

— *Ruth Guthrie Harding*

&

I was more true to Love
than Love to me.

— *anonymous*

è•

Familiar acts are beautiful through love.
— *Percy Bysshe Shelley*
(1792–1822) English poet

è•

There is no fear in love
perfect love casteth out fear.
— *1 John 4:18*

è•

Oh, the miraculous energy
that flows between two people
who care enough to take the risks
of responding with the whole heart.
— *Alex Noble*

è•

The power to love truly and devoutly
is the noblest gift,
which a human being can be endowed.
— *Geraldine Endsor*

ह⋑

All my heart to you
with love and kisses.

—unknown

ह⋑

Love understands,
and therefore waits.

— F. Drummond

ह⋑

People who are sensible about love
are incapable of it.

— Douglas Yates

ह⋑

Love is the master key
that opens the gates of happiness.

— Oliver Wendell Holmes
(1809-1894) American poet

ह⋑

True love...
The silver link, the silver tie, which heart to heart,
and mind to mind, in body and in soul can bind.

— Sir Walter Scott
(1771-1832) Scottish poet/novelist

❧

There is only one happiness in life,
to love and be loved.
— *George Sand*
(1804-1876) French writer

❧

Love is a canvas furnished by nature
and embroidered by imagination.
— *François-Marie Arouet de Voltaire*
(1694-1778) French philosophical writer

❧

Love...is like a beautiful flower
which I may not touch, but
whose fragrance makes the
garden a place of delight just the same.
— *Helen Keller*
(1880-1968) blind/deaf American writer

❧

Our love must not be a thing
of words and fine talk.
It must be a thing
of action and sincerity.
— *1 John 3:18*

ॐ

We can do no great things;
only small things with great love.
— *Mother Teresa*
(1910-1997) Yugoslavian Roman Catholic missionary

ॐ

Doubt that the stars are fire;
Doubt that the sun doth move;
Doubt truth to be a liar;
But never doubt I love.
— *William Shakespeare*
(1564-1616) English writer

ॐ

There isn't any formula or method.
You learn to love by doing.
— *Aldous Huxley*
(1894-1963) English novelist

ॐ

Love is never lost.
If not reciprocated
it will flow back and soften and purify the heart.
— *Washington Irving*
(1703-1859) American essayist

❧

Love opens the door into everything,
as far as I can see, including and perhaps most of all,
the door into one's own secret,
and often terrible and frightening,
real self.

— *May Sarton*

❧

If we want a love message to be heard,
it has to be sent.
To keep a lamp burning,
we have to keep putting oil in it.

— *Mother Teresa*
(1910-1997) Yugoslavian Roman Catholic missionary

❧

Love is everything it's cracked up to be.
That's why people are so cynical about it...
It really is worth fighting for,
being brave for, risking everything for.
And the trouble is, if you don't risk anything,
you risk even more.

— *Erica Jong*
(1942-) American writer

❧

Love is both the task
and the reward.

— *Jane Smiley*

❧

Love means
exposing yourself to the pain of being hurt,
deeply hurt by someone you trust.

— *Renita Weems*

❧

Love is indescribable and unconditional.
I could tell you a thousand things that it is not,
but not one that it is.

— *Duke Ellington*

(1899-1974) American jazz pianist/composer

❧

Until I truly loved,
I was alone.

— *Caroline Sheridan Norton*

❧

Start and Goal
What is the beginning? Love.
What is the course? Love still.
What the goal? the goal is Love
On the happy hill.
Is there nothing then but Love?
Search we sky or earth.
There is nothing out of Love
Hath perpetual worth;
All things flag but only Love,
All things fail and flee;
There is nothing left but Love
Worthy you and me.

— Christina Rossetti
(1830-1894) English poet

❧

You have become a necessity of my life,
and you will drive me mad,
not only if you will not love me,
but if you will not let me love you.

— Alexandre Dumas
(1802-1870) French novelist

❧

It has been said that we need just three things in life:
Something to do,
Something to look forward to.
And someone to love.

— *unknown*

❧

Love is all we have,
the only way that each can help the other.

— *Euripides*
(485-406 BC) Greek tragic dramatist

❧

A true lover is one to whom you can pour out the
contents of your heart, chaff and grain alike.
Knowing that the gentlest of hands will take and sift
it, keep what is worth keeping and with a breath of
kindness, blow the rest away.

— *unknown*

❧

Take this heart of mine
into your hands.

— *Laforrest Cope*

❧

One word frees us of all the weight and pain of life:
That word is love.
— *Sophocles*
(496–406 BC) Athenian dramatic poet

❧

Love doesn't make the world go 'round.
Love is what makes the ride worthwhile.
— *Franklin P. Jones*

❧

Love doesn't just sit there, like a stone;
it has to be made, like bread,
remade all the time, made new.
— *Ursula K. Le Guin*
(1929-) American writer

❧

...Love is not a clock.
You simply cannot take it apart
just to see what makes it tick,
and even if you could,
you probably could never
get it back together again.
— *anonymous*

🐦

To be able to say how much love is to love but little.
— *Petrarch*

🐦

Brevity may be the soul of wit, but not when
someone's saying, "I love you."
— *Judith Viorst*

🐦

But that our loves and comforts should increase, even
as our days do grow.
— *William Shakespeare*
(1564-1616) English writer

🐦

Two hearts that love make one divine.
The light they yield shall ever shine.
— *Elizabeth Barrett Browning*
(1806-1861) English poet

🐦

Harvest the love you have planted.
— *unknown*

આ

I have poured out all my troubles.
None of them matters,
when I think of you.
— *Edna St. Vincent Millay*
(1892-1950) American poet

આ

I tell you my dreams and
while you're listening to me,
I suddenly see them come true.
— *Alan Jay Lerner*

આ

You're the light that shines within me,
guiding me through.
— *Leslie Bricusse*

આ

Falling in love consists merely in uncorking the
imagination and bottling the common-sense.
— *Helen Rowland*

❧

I sleep soundly, safely enfolded
in the light of your love.

— *unknown*

❧

You are the light of my life.
Your bright heart warms my soul.

— *unknown*

❧

Love:
its influence, thrown in our eyes,
genders a novel sense,
at which we start and fret;
till in the end, melting into its radiance,
we blend, mingle, and so become a part of it.

— *John Keats*
(1795-1821) English poet

❧

What orbit of the planets has put you and me in this
place, at this moment? Where time takes a breath,
and we dance on the edge of our dreams?

— *unknown*

❧

I love you because it would be impossible
for me not to love you.
— *Juliette Drouet*

❧

I never know what to think of you...
what makes your mystery...your charm.
— *unknown*

❧

It's like you took my dreams
and made each one real.
You reached inside of me
and made me feel.
— *Leslie Bricusse*

❧

Love is cruel, and selfish, and totally obtuse—
at least, blinded by the light, young love is.
But we have, no matter how, by our wills,
survived to keep the jeweled prize at our fingertips
we will it so, and so it is past all accident.
— *William Carlos Williams*
(1883–1963) American poet/writer

&

Your love has opened every door.
Now, I can soar!
— *Leslie Bricusse*

&

Life is for joy, for giving,
for sharing and for laughter,
but mostly—it's for love.

— *unknown*

&

When I gaze into your eyes
Then sorrow passes; I grow wise;
And when I kiss your lips so red
All pain is changed to joy instead.
— *Heinrich Heine*
(1797-1856) German Jewish poet

&

The greatest love is that we know,
When life is just an afterglow.
— *Georgia Douglas Johnson*

❧

Traveling in the company of those we love
is home in motion.
— *Leigh Hunt*
(1784-1859) English critic/essayist

❧

Love is the only flower that grows and blossoms
without the aid of seasons.
— *Kahlil Gibran*
(1883-1931) Lebanonese poet/philosopher

❧

Love builds the house on rock and not on sand.
Love laughs while the winds rave desperately.
— *Christina Rossetti*
(1830-1894) English poet

❧

For love is a celestial harmony
of likely hearts composed of stars; consent,
which join together in sweet sympathy,
to work each other's joy and true content.
— *Edmund Spenser*
(1552-1599) English poet

❧

Security is a sense of staying put,
but love is always in motion.
— *Michael Ventura*

❧

Love develops deep within you.
It grows and is constantly changing.
— *Flavia*

❧

It is as if, in the complex language of love,
there were a word that could be spoken by lips
when lips touch, a silent contract sealed with a kiss.
— *Diane Ackerman*

❧

When I send thee a red, red rose,—
The sweetest flower on earth that grows!
Think, dear heart, how I love thee;...
— *Friedrich Rückert*
(1788-1866) German poet

❧

We cannot really love anybody
with whom we never laugh.
— *Agnes Repplier*

❧

Love makes us "heavenly" without
our trying in the least.
— *Emily Dickinson*
(1830–1886) American poet

❧

I love you with unchanged
and unchangeable affection,
and while I retain your friendship,
I retain the best that life has given me.
— *Marian Evans*

❧

There is no harvest for the heart alone.
The seed of love must be Eternally resown.
— *Anne Morrow Lindbergh*
(1906–) American writer/aviator

❧

You may fall from a tree-top.
You may fall from above.
But the greatest fall you'll ever have
is when you fall in love.
— *Susan J. Gordon*

≥●

They came to tell your faults to me.
They named them over one by one.
I laughed aloud when they were done.
I knew them all so well before—
Oh, they were blind, too blind to see.
Your faults had made me love you more.

— *Sara Teasdale*
(1884–1933) American poet

≥●

You are tied to my heart by a cord
which can never be broken
and which really pulls me continually.
My love for you rests on a past
which no future can reverse.

— *Marian Evans*

≥●

'Tis you that are the music, not your song.
The song is but a door which, opening wide,
lets forth the pent-up melody inside your spirit's
harmony which, clear and strong, sings but of you.

— *Amy Lowell*
(1874–1925) American poet

❧

'Twas not into my ear you whispered
but into my heart.

— *Judy Garland*
(1922-1969) American singer/actress

❧

To love a person
is to learn the song that is in their heart,
and sing it to them when they have forgotten.

— *Thomas Chandler*

❧

In well-cool hollow your way,
in bee-soft bower sleep you.
In drift, in dream, drink fresh, breathe free;
in dream in home, love keep you.

— *Mary Phelps*

❧

If you have love in your life it can
make up for a great many things that are missing.
If you don't have love in your life,
no matter what else there is, it's not enough.

— *Ann Landers*

&

I have not spent a day without loving you.
— *Napoleon Bonaparte*
(1769–1821) French general/leader

&

Whoever lives true life will love true love.
— *Elizabeth Barrett Browning*
(1806–1861) English poet

&

The greatest happiness
is the conviction that we are loved,
loved for ourselves,
or rather loved in spite of ourselves.
— *Victor Hugo*
(1802–1885) French romantic poet/novelist

&

The longer we love...
the stronger we love.
— *e. b. michaels*

Thou wilt not love to live,
unless thou live to love.
— *Edmund Spenser*
(1552-1599) English poet

I love you because
you are you.
— *Michel Eyquem de Montaigne*
(1533-1592) French writer/philosopher

I'm not easy to understand,
but you hold out your hand
and you say you love me
just as I am.
— *Bob Hegel & Dick Warner*

Love is a song that never ends;
one simple theme repeating.
Like the voice of a heavenly choir,
love's sweet music goes on.
— *Larry Morey*

è&

I love you and live, or...
I merely exist.
— *William Carlos Williams*
(1883-1963) American poet/writer

è&

Long ago, with love's bands,
you bound me.
— *Christina Rossetti*
(1830-1894) English poet

è&

I never knew that I could feel such wonder.
I never knew that love could be like this.
— *Leslie Bricusse*

è&

What a curious thing love is;
only a sentiment, and yet
it has the power to make fools of men
and slaves of women.
— *Louisa May Alcott*
(1832-1888) American writer
Long & Fatal Chase

❧

Love is the attempt
to change a piece of a dream-
world into reality.
— *Theodor Reik*

❧

Love is the falling rain,
Love is the following flood,
And love is the ark
With two of a kind aboard.
— *Barbara Deming*

❧

Love is the most terrible,
and also the most generous of the passions;
it is the only one which includes in its dreams
the happiness of someone else.
— *Alphonse Karr*

❧

Love is the wine of existence.
— *Henry Ward Beecher*

ॐ

We can only learn to love by loving.
— *Iris Murdoch*
(1919–) Irish novelist/philosopher

ॐ

If Love

If love were what the rose is,
And I were like the leaf,
Our lives would grow together
In sad or singing weather,
Blown fields or flowerful closes,
Green pleasure or grey grief;
If love were what the rose is,
And I were like the leaf.
— *Algernon Charles Swinburne*
(1837–1909) English poet

ॐ

Love is a rain of diamonds in the mind.
— *May Swenson*

ॐ

Love is spiritual fire.
— *Emanuel Swedenborg*
(1688–1772) Swedish scientist/philosopher

Love is the life of the soul.
It is the harmony of the universe.
— *William Ellery Channing*
(1780-1842) American clergyman

Love is the only thing you get more of
by giving it away.
— *Tom Wilson*

Love is the blinding revelation
that some other being can be more important
to the lover than he is to himself.
— *J. V. Casserley*

Love is, above all,
the gift of oneself.
— *Jean Anouilh*
(1910-1987) French dramatist

ॐ

How do I love thee? Let me count the ways.
I love thee to the depth and breadth and height
My soul can reach, when feeling out of sight
For the ends of Being and ideal Grace.
I love thee to the level of every day's
Most quiet need, by sun and candlelight.
I love thee freely, as men strive for right;
I love thee purely, as they turn from praise.
I love thee with the passion put to use
In my old briefs, and with my childhood's faith.
I love thee with a love I seemed to lose
With my lost saints—I love thee with the breath,
Smiles, tears, of all my life!—and, if God choose,
I shall but love thee better after death.
— *Elizabeth Barrett Browning*
(1806-1861) English poet
Sonnets from the Portuguese

ॐ

Love is an irresistible desire
to be irresistibly desired.
— *Robert Frost*
(1874-1963) American poet

We love because it's the only true adventure.
— *Nikki Giovanni*

What is love?
Two souls and one flesh.
— *Joseph Roux*

Remember that happiness is a way of travel,
not a destination.
— *Roy Goodman*

A human being loves another,
because he is who and what he is;
he seeks the other's own self;
he seeks what makes the other
this particular individual person.
To love means to say:
it is good that you are you,
it is very good.
— *Ladislaus Boros*

❧

Till I loved
I never loved—enough.
— *Emily Dickinson*
(1830-1886) American poet

❧

We seek the comfort of another.
Someone to share and share the life we choose.
Someone to help us through the never ending
attempt to understand ourselves. And in the end,
someone to comfort us along the way.
— *Marlin Finch Lupus*

❧

Love is an emotion experienced by the many
and enjoyed by the few.
— *George Jean Nathan*
(1882-1958) American critic/author

❧

When love and skill work together,
expect a masterpiece.
— *John Ruskin*
(1819-1900) English art critic/essayist

ॐ

Love is Enough

Love is enough: though the World be a-waning,
And the woods have no voice
but the voice of complaining,
Though the skies be too dark for dim eyes to discover
The gold-cups and daisies fair blooming thereunder,
Though the hills be held shadows,
and the sea a dark wonder,
And this day draw a veil over all deeds pass'd over,
Yet their hands shall not tremble,
their feet shall not falter:
The void shall not weary the fear shall not alter
These lips and these eyes of the loved and the lover.

— *William Barry Morris*
(1834-1896) English poet

ॐ

You will suffer,
and if you do not love,
you do not know the meaning of a Christian life.

— *Agatha Christie*
(1890-1976) English mystery writer

ॐ

If ever Two were One

If ever two were one, then surely we.
If ever man were loved by wife, then thee;
If ever wife was happy in a man,
Compare with me, ye women, if you can.
I prize thy love more than whole mines of gold
Or all the riches that the East doth hold.
My love is such that rivers cannot quench,
Nor ought but love from thee, give recompense.
Thy love is such I can no way repay,
The heavens reward thee manifold, I pray
Then while we live, in love let's so preserve
That when we live no more, we may live ever.

— *Anne Bradstreet*
(1612-1672) American poet

ॐ

The lover and the physician
are each popular for the same cause—
we talk to them of nothing but ourselves.

— *L. E. Landon*

❧

They who love are but
one step from heaven.
— *James Russell Lowell*
(1819-1892) American writer

❧

We are shaped and fashioned by what we love.
— *Johann Wolfgang von Goethe*
(1749-1832) German poet/novelist

❧

Love isn't like a reservoir.
You'll never drain it dry.
It's much more like a natural spring.
The longer and the farther it flows,
the stronger and the deeper and
the clearer it becomes.
— *Eddie Cantor*

❧

It is astonishing how little one feels poverty
when one loves.
— *John Bulwer*

❧

If it is your time,
love will track you down
like a cruise missile.

— Lynda Barry

❧

ARDOR, n. The quality that distinguishes
love without knowledge.

— Ambrose Bierce
(1842-1914) American satirist
The Devil's Dictionary, 1911

❧

LOVE, n. A temporary insanity
curable by marriage
or by removal of the patient
from the influences under which
he incurred the disorder...
It is sometimes fatal,
but more frequently to the physician
than to the patient.

— Ambrose Bierce
(1842-1914) American satirist
The Devil's Dictionary, 1911

ਟ&

Love is shown in your deeds,
not in your words.
— *Fr. Jerome Cummings*

ਟ&

The way to love anything
is to realize that it might be lost.
— *Gilbert Keith Chesterton*
(1874-1936) English novelist/essayist

ਟ&

There is only one kind of love,
but there are a thousand imitations.
— *François, Duc de La Rochefoucauld*
(1613-1680) French writer

ਟ&

Honor the ocean of love.
— *George de Benneville*

❧

Love is an ocean of emotions
entirely surrounded by expenses.
— *Sir James Dewar*
(1842–1923) Scottish chemist/physicist

❧

Immature love says:
"I love you because I need you."
Mature love says:
"I need you because I love you."
— *Erich Fromm*
(1900–) German psychoanalyst

❧

Love is the greatest beautifier
in the universe.
— *May Christie*

❧

People need loving the most
when they deserve it the least.
— *John Harrigan*

An act of love that fails
is just as much a part of the divine life
as an act of love that succeeds,
for love is measured by fullness,
not by reception.
— *Harold Loukes*

Love is like pi —
natural, irrational, and very important.
— *Lisa Hoffman*

Life is the flower for which love is the honey.
— *Victor Hugo*
(1802-1885) French romantic poet/novelist

Love, I find, is like singing.
Everybody can do enough to satisfy themselves,
though it may not impress the neighbors as
being very much.
— *Zora Neale Hurston*

🖾

Love is the great miracle cure.
Loving ourselves works miracles in our lives.
— *Louise Hay*

🖾

For the memory of love is sweet,
though the love itself were in vain.
And what I have lost of pleasure,
assuages what I find of pain.

— *Lyster*

🖾

Love is an emotion that is based on an opinion of
women that is impossible for those who have had
any experience with them.
— *Henry Louis Mencken*
(1880-1956) American editor

🖾

It is with true love as it is with ghosts;
everyone talks about it,
but few have seen it.
— *François, Duc de La Rochefoucauld*
(1613-1680) French writer

❧

Love cures people, both the ones who give it
and the ones who receive it.
— *Dr. Karl Menninger*
(1893–) American psychiatrist

❧

Nothing takes the taste out of peanut butter
quite like unrequited love.
— *Charlie Brown*
"Peanuts" comic strip, created by Charles Schultz

❧

It is wrong to think that love comes from long
companionship and persevering courtship. Love is the
offspring of spiritual affinity and unless that affinity is
created in a moment, it will not be created for years
or even generations.
— *Kahlil Gibran*
(1883–1931) Lebanonese poet/philosopher

❧

Love is the delusion that one man or woman
differs from another.
— *Henry Louis Mencken*
(1880–1956) American editor

❧

Love is the flower of life,
and blossoms unexpectedly and without law,
and must be plucked where it is found,
and enjoyed for the brief hour of its duration.
— *David Herbert Lawrence*
(1855-1930) English writer

❧

Age does not protect you from love
but love to some extent protects you from age.
— *Jeanne Moreau*

❧

Love is like the measles.
The older you are when you get it,
the worse the attack.
— *Mary Roberts Rhinehart*

❧

Love is blind—
marriage is the eye-opener.
— *Pauline Thomason*

This is the miracle that happens every time
to those who really love;
the more they give,
the more they possess.

— *Rainer Maria Rilke*
(1875-1926) Austro-German poet

To write a good love letter,
you ought to begin without knowing
what you mean to say,
and to finish without knowing
what you have written.

— *Jean-Jacques Rousseau*
(1712-1778) French philosopher/novelist

Love looks not with the eyes,
but with the mind;
And therefore is winged
Cupid painted blind.

— *William Shakespeare*
(1564-1616) English writer
A Midsummer-Night's Dream

I have found the paradox that if I love until it hurts,
then there is no hurt, but only more love.

— Mother Teresa
(1910-1997) Yugoslavian Roman Catholic missionary

If love is the answer,
could you rephrase the question?

— Lily Tomlin
(1939-) comedienne/actress

Love is much nicer to be in than an automobile
accident, a tight girdle, a higher tax bracket, or a
holding pattern over Philadelphia.

— Judith Viorst

Love is a gross exaggeration of the difference
between one person and everybody else.

— George Bernard Shaw
(1856-1950) Irish dramatist

❧

Who, being loved, is poor?

— *Oscar Wilde*
(1854-1900) Irish poet/essayist

❧

Miracles occur naturally as expressions of love.
The real miracle is the love that inspires them.
In this sense everything that comes from love
is a miracle.

— *Marianne Williamson*

❧

Love seeketh not itself to please,
Nor for itself hath any care,
But for another gives it ease,
And builds a Heaven in Hell's despair.

— *William Blake*
(1757-1827) English poet/artist

❧

May we always love each other...
as we are, not as we were.

— *Michael Macfarlane*

To fall in love is to create a religion
that has a fallible god.
— *Jorge Luis Borges*
(1899-1980) *Argentinian writer*

Love is the same as like
except you feel sexier.
— *Judith Viorst*

The mark of a true crush...is that you fall in love first
and grope for reasons afterward.
— *Shana Alexander*

Love—what a volume in a word,
an ocean in a tear,
A seventh heaven in a glance,
a whirlwind in a sigh.
The lightning in a touch,
a millennium in a moment.
— *M. F. Tupper*

૨૭

Love shortens time,
charms the hours.
Love is invincible.
Many waters cannot quench it,
nor the floods drown.
The supreme happiness of life
is the conviction that we are loved.
Love, indeed,
lends a precious seeing to the eye,
and hearing to the ear:
all sights and sounds are glorified
by the light of its presence.
— *Fredrick Saunders*

૨૭

Love is sweetest seasoned with respect.
— *George Clifford*

૨૭

Some pray to marry the man they love,
My prayer will somewhat vary:
I humbly pray to Heaven above
That I love the man I marry.
— *Rose Pastor Stokes*

ès

Love is what we are born with.
Fear is what we learn.
The spiritual journey is the unlearning of fear
and prejudices and the acceptance of love
back in our hearts.
Love is the essential reality
and our purpose on earth.
To be consciously aware of it,
to experience love in ourselves and others,
is the meaning of life.
Meaning does not lie in things.
Meaning lies in us.
— *Marianne Williamson*
A Return to Love

ès

May our love be perfect, even if we are not.
— *Michael Macfarlane*

ès

O what a heaven is love!
O what a hell!
— *Thomas Dekker*

❧

Life has taught us that love
does not consist in gazing at each other
but in looking outward together
in the same direction.
— *Antoine de Saint-Exupery*

❧

Love is the child of illusion
and the parent of disillusion.
— *Miguel de Unamuno*
(1864–1936) Spanish philosopher

❧

I am two fools, I know,
For loving, and for saying so in
Whining poetry.

— *John Donne*
(1572–1631) English poet

❧

Love is an ideal thing,
marriage a real thing;
a confusion of the real
with the ideal never goes unpunished.
— *Johann Wolfgang von Goethe*
(1749–1832) German poet/novelist

❧

Love never reasons, but profusely gives;
gives, like a thoughtless prodigal, its all,
and trembles then lest it has done too little.

— *Hannah More*
(1745-1833) English writer

❧

To love and be loved
is to feel the sun from both sides.

— *David Viscott*

❧

Love is like a garden.
It will continue to grow wild
but flourishes best with attention.
May your garden always remain in full bloom.

— *unknown*

❧

Had we never loved so blindly
Had we never looked so kindly
Never met—or never parted
We would not be now so broken hearted.

— *unknown*

ॐ

Two little boys were playing together
when a cute, curly-haired girl walked by.
"You know something?
When I stop hating girls,
I think I'll stop hating that one first!"

— *unknown*

ॐ

And remember guys:
while sex using a condom
may be like taking a shower in a raincoat,
sex without a condom
is like taking a bath with the toaster.

— *unknown*

ॐ

Here's to Eve, Mother of our race,
Who wore a fig leaf in the right place.
And to Adam, Father of us all,
Who was Johnny-on-the-spot
when the leaves began to fall!

— *unknown*

❧

Did you hear about the bachelor who
put on a pair of clean socks every day?
At the end of the week he couldn't get his shoes on.
— *unknown*

❧

FOR SALE BY OWNER
Complete set of Encyclopedia Britannica.
45 volumes. Excellent condition.
$1,000.00 or best offer. No longer needed.
Got married last weekend. Wife knows everything.
— *New York Times*

❧

A little boy asked his father,
"Daddy, how much does it cost to get married?"
And the father replied,
"I don't know son, I'm still paying."
— *unknown*

❧

Those who love deeply never grow old;
they may die of old age, but they die young.
Sir Arthur Wing Pinero
(1855-1934) English dramatist

❧

Getting married is very much like
going to a restaurant with friends.
You order what you want,
then when you see what the other person has,
you wish you had ordered that.

— *unknown*

❧

At the cocktail party, one woman said to another,
"Aren't you wearing your wedding ring
on the wrong finger.
The other replied, "Yes I am,
I married the wrong man."

— *unknown*

❧

A lady inserted an 'ad' in the classifieds:
"Husband wanted."
Next day she received a hundred letters.
They all said the same thing:
"You can have mine."

— *unknown*

❧

After a quarrel, a husband said to his wife,
"You know, I was a fool when I married you."
She replied, "Yes, dear,
but I was in love and didn't notice."

— *unknown*

❧

If you want your spouse to listen
and pay strict attention
to every word you say,
talk in your sleep.

— *unknown*

❧

Love me or hate me,
but spare me your indifference.

— *Libbie Fudim*

❧

True love comes quietly,
without banners or flashing lights.
If you hear bells,
get your ears checked.

— *Erich Segal*

❧

There are people whom one
loves immediately and forever.
Even to know they are alive in the world
with one is quite enough.
— *Nancy Spain*

❧

Infatuation is when you think that he's
as sexy as Robert Redford,
as smart as Henry Kissinger,
as noble as Ralph Nader,
as funny as Woody Allen,
and as athletic as Jimmy Conners.
Love is when you realize that he's
as sexy as Woody Allen, as
smart as Jimmy Conners,
as funny as Ralph Nader,
as athletic as Henry Kissinger,
and nothing like Robert Redford—
but you'll take him anyway.
— *Judith Viorst*

❧

Love is the answer,
but while you're waiting for the answer,
sex raises some pretty good questions.

— *Woody Allen*
(1935-) American actor/writer

❧

Love is a fire.
But whether it is going to warm your hearth
or burn down your house,
you can never tell.

— *Joan Crawford*
American actress

❧

Love, in present day society,
is just the exchange of two momentary desires
and the contact of two skins.

— *Nicolas Chamfort*

❧

Sex: the thing that takes up the least amount of time
and causes the most amount of trouble.

— *John Barrymore*
(1882-1942) American actor

&

It is most unwise for people
in love to marry.
— *George Bernard Shaw*
(1856-1950) Irish dramatist

&

It is better to be hated for what
you are than to be loved for what you are not.
— *André Gide*
(1869-1951) French novelist

&

Love and work
are the cornerstones of our humanness.
— *Sigmund Freud*
(1856-1939) Austrian psychoanalyst

&

True, we love life, not because we are used to living,
but because we are used to loving.
There is always some madness in love,
but there is also always some reason in madness.
— *Friedrich W. Nietzsche*
(1844-1900) German philosopher

≈

I want to tell you a terrific story about contraception.
I asked this girl to sleep with me,
and she said "no."

— *Woody Allen*
(1935-) *American actor/writer*

≈

The ability to make love frivolously
is the chief characteristic which
distinguishes human beings from beasts.

— *Heywood Broun*
(1888-1939) *American journalist*

≈

When we want to read of the deeds
that are done for love,
whither do we turn?
To the murder column.

— *George Bernard Shaw*
(1856-1950) *Irish dramatist*

≈

The fate of love is that it always
seems too little or too much.

— *Amelia E. Barr*

❧

Accept the things to which fate binds you, and love
the people with whom fate brings you together,
but do so with all your heart.
— *Marcus Aurelius*

❧

Beware you be not swallowed up in books!
An ounce of love is worth a pound of knowledge.
— *John Wesley*
(1703-1791) English clergyman

❧

When angry, count to a hundred.
— *Mark Twain*
(1834-1910) American novelist

❧

Tact is the art of making a point
without making an enemy.
The most difficult thing in the world
is to know how to do a thing
and to watch someone else
doing it wrong and keep quiet.
— *Benjamin Franklin*
(1706-1790) American scientist/statesman

ᘒ

I have come to the conclusion
never again to think of marrying, and for this reason,
I can never be satisfied with anyone
who would be blockhead enough to have me.
— *Abraham Lincoln*
(1809-1865) 16th American president
in a letter to Mrs. O.H. Browning, April 1, 1838

ᘒ

To err is human; to forgive divine.
Education forms the common mind;
Just as the twig is bent, the tree's inclined.
— *Alexander Pope*
(1688-1744) English poet

ᘒ

Bachelors know more about women
than married men;
if they didn't,
they'd be married too.
— *Henry Louis Mencken*
(1880-1956) American editor

❧

Be thou familiar, but by no means vulgar...
Costly thy habit as they purse can buy.
But not expressed in fancy; rich, not gaudy,
For the apparel oft proclaims the man.
Neither a borrower nor a lender be,
For oft the loan loses both itself and a friend,
And borrowing dulls the edge of husbandry.
This above all: to thine own self be true,
And it must follow, as the night the day,
Thou canst not then be false to any man.
Farewell, my blessing season this in thee.
— *William Shakespeare*
(1564–1616) English writer
Hamlet

❧

To say the words "love and compassion" is easy.
But to accept that love and compassion are built
upon patience and perseverance is not easy.
Your marriage will be firm and lasting
if you remember this.
— *Buddhist marriage homily*

❧

The big difference between
sex for money
and sex for free
is that sex for money
usually costs a lot less.
— *Bendan Francis*

❧

Women don't smoke after sex
because one drag a night is enough.
— *anonymous*

❧

Sex is like money—
very nicc to have
but vulgar to talk about.
— *Tonia Berg*

❧

Sex is like pizza.
Even when it's bad,
it's still pretty good.
— *Helen Childress*

❧

Sex is like having dinner;
sometimes you joke about the dishes,
sometimes you take the meal seriously.
— *Woody Allen*
(1935-) American actor/writer

❧

A promiscuous person is someone
who is getting more sex than you are.
— *Victor Lownes*

❧

Love is not enough.
It must be the foundation, the cornerstone—
but not the complete structure.
— *Bette Davis*
American actress

❧

You know, she speaks eighteen languages.
And she can't say 'no' in any of them.
— *Dorothy Parker*
(1893-) American satirist

❧

Whoever named it necking
was a poor judge of anatomy.

— *Groucho Marx*
(1891-1977) comedian

❧

People who throw kisses
are hopelessly lazy.

— *Bob Hope*
(1903-) American actor/comedian

❧

All this fuss about sleeping together
for physical pleasure.
I'd sooner go to my dentist any day.

— *Evelyn Waugh*
(1903-1966) English novelist/satirist

❧

Chastity:
the most unnatural of the sexual perversions.

— *Aldous Huxley*
(1894-1963) English novelist

❧

Understand, I'll slip quietly
away from the noisy crowd
when I see the pale
stars rising, blooming, over the oaks.
I'll pursue solitary pathways
through the pale twilit meadows,
with only this one dream:
You come too.

— *Rainer Maria Rilke*
(1875-1926) Austro-German poet

❧

Oh, I am thinking
Oh, I am thinking
I have found my lover.
Oh, I think it is so.

— *Chippewa song*

❧

Ask yourself my love
whether you are not very cruel
to have so entrammelled me,
so destroyed my freedom.

— *John Keats*
(1795-1821) English poet

❧

It is love, not reason, that is stronger than death.
— *Thomas Mann*
(1875-1955) German novelist

❧

Everyone admits that love is wonderful
and necessary, yet no one agrees on just what it is.
— *Diane Ackerman*

❧

The Eskimo has fifty-two names for snow
because it is important to them;
there ought to be as many for love.
— *Margaret Atwood*

❧

Winter twilight
On a window pane
I write your name.
— *Japanese haiku*

❧

Love and a cough cannot be hidden.
— *Japanese proverb*

I have loved, and bitterness left me for an hour.
But there are times when love itself is bitter.

— *Agnes Smedley*

Oh, love is real enough,
you will find it some day,
but it has one arch-enemy—
and that is life.

— *Jean Anouilh*
(1910-1987) French dramatist

Absence is to love what wind is to fire; it
extinguishes the small, it enkindles the great.

— *Comte de Bussy-Rabutin*

Love must be learned, and learned again and again.
Hate needs no instructions,
but waits only to be provoked.

— *Katherine Anne Porter*
(1890-1980) American writer

George will work in your thoughts till you die.
It isn't possible to love and to part.
You will wish that it was.
You can transmute love, ignore it, muddle it,
but you can never pull it out of you...love is eternal...
I only wish poets would say this, too:
love is of the body; not the body but of the body.
Ah! the misery that would be saved if we confessed
that!...When I think what life is and how seldom love
is answered by love — Marry him;
it is one of the moments
for which the world was made...

— *E. M. Forster*
(1879-1970) English novelist
A Room With A View

There are truly only
four questions that matter:
What is sacred,
Of what is the spirit made,
What is worth living for,
And what is worth dying for?
The answer to all of these is love.

— *unknown*

What thou lov'st well remains, the rest is dross
What thou lov'st well shall not be reft from thee
What thou lov'st well is thy true heritage...
— *Ezra Pound*
(1885-1972) American poet/critic

Love is a battle. Love is war. Love is growing up.
— *James Baldwin*
(1861-1934) American psychologist/educator

In the marriage ceremony,
that moment when falling in love is replaced by the
arduous drama of staying in love,
the words "in sickness and in health,
for richer, for poorer, till death do us part"
set love in the temporal context
in which it achieves its meaning.
As time begins to elapse, one begins to love the
other because they have shared the same
experience... Selves may not intertwine; but lives do,
and shared memory becomes as much of a bond as
the bond of the flesh...
— *Michael Ignatieff*

ॐ

The moment I heard my first love story I began
seeking you, not realizing the search was useless.
Lovers don't meet somewhere along the way.
They're in one another's souls from the beginning.

— *Jalal al-din Rumi*
Persian love poem

ॐ

I will reveal to you a love potion, without medicine,
without herbs, without any witch's magic;
if you want to be loved, the Love.

— *Hecaton of Rhodes*

ॐ

Upon my soul I have loved you to the extreme.

— *John Keats*
(1795-1821) English poet

ॐ

Is there in any land
any man whom you love
more than you love me?

— *unknown*

❧

I would go anywhere
to take you in my arms
again, my darling.

— *Sappho*
(620-565 BC) Greek lyric poet

❧

I have placed my head and my heart
On the sill of the door of my love.
Step gently, child!

— *Turkoman love song*

❧

When one has good wine,
a graceful boat,
and a maiden's love,
why envy the immortal gods?

— *Li Tai Po*
Song on the River

❧

Safe now. I've flown to you
like a child to its mother.

— *unknown*

Man

೭ঌ

He believes that marriage and a career don't mix.
So after the wedding he plans to quit his job.
— *anonymous*

೭ঌ

If it weren't for marriage, men would spend their
lives thinking they had no faults at all.
— *anonymous*

೭ঌ

The theory used to be you marry an older man
because they are more mature.
The new theory is that men don't mature.
So you might as well marry a younger one.
— *anonymous*

೭ঌ

Some men are born with cold feet;
some acquire cold feet;
and some have cold feet thrust upon them.
— *anonymous*

In the past decade or so, the women's magazines have taken to running home-handyperson articles suggesting that women can learn to fix things just as well as men. These articles are apparently based on the ludicrous assumption that men know how to fix things, when in fact all they know how to do is look at things in a certain squinty-eyed manner, which they learned in Wood Shop; eventually, when enough things in the home are broken, they take a job requiring them to transfer to another home.

— *Dave Barry*

The male is a domestic animal which, if treated with firmness, can be trained to do most things.

— *Jilly Cooper*

Many a man that could rule a hundred million strangers with an ir'n hand is careful to take off his shoes in the front hallway when he comes home late at night.

— *Finley Peter Dunne*
(1867-1936) American humorist
Mr. Dooley On Making A Will, 1919

ॐ

Beware of men on airplanes.
The minute a man reaches thirty thousand feet,
he immediately becomes consumed by distasteful
sexual fantasies which involve doing uncomfortable
things in those tiny toilets.
These men should not be encouraged,
their fantasies are sadly low-rent and unimaginative.
Affect an aloof, cool demeanor as soon as
any man tries to draw you out.
Unless, of course, he's the pilot.

— *Cynthia Heimel*

ॐ

If God wanted women to understand men,
football would never have been created.

— *unknown*

ॐ

A man when he is making up to anybody can be
cordial and gallant and full of little attentions and
altogether charming. But when a man is really in love
he can't help looking like a sheep.

— *Agatha Christie*
(1890-1976) English mystery writer

❦

Women want mediocre men,
and men are working hard to become
as mediocre as possible.
— *Margaret Mead*
(1901-1978) American anthropologist

❦

The best way to hold a man
is in your arms.
— *Mae West*
(1892-1980) American actress

❦

Man is a natural polygamist.
He always has one woman leading him by the nose
and another hanging on to his coattails.
— *Henry Louis Mencken*
(1880-1956) American editor

❦

It's a funny thing that when a man hasn't got
anything on earth to worry about,
he goes off and gets married.
— *Robert Frost*
(1874-1963) American poet

৵

A great man is he who has not
lost the heart of a child.

— *Mencius*

(372-289 BC) Chinese philosopher

৵

A man should be taller, older,
heavier, uglier, and hoarser than his wife.

— *Edgar Watson Howe*

৵

The more I know about men, the more I like dogs.

— *Gloria Allred*

৵

The young man who wants to marry happily
should pick out a good mother
and marry one of her daughters...
any one will do.

— *Jonathan Ogden Armour*

(1863-1927) American meat packing innovator

৵

Plenty of guys are good at sex,
but conversation: now there's an art.

— *Linda Barnes*

৶

Men always want to be a woman's first love—
women like to be a man's last romance.
— *Oscar Wilde*
(1854-1900) Irish poet/essayist

৶

Men have a much better time of it than women:
for one thing they marry later,
for another thing they die earlier.
— *Henry Louis Mencken*
(1880-1956) American editor

৶

A gentleman is a man who can disagree
without being disagreeable.
— *anonymous*

৶

Marrying a man is like
buying something you've been admiring
for a long time in a shop window.
You may love it when you get it home,
but it doesn't always go
with everything in the house.
— *Jean Kerr*

❧

He's the kind of man
a woman would have to marry
to get rid of.

— *Mae West*
(1892-1980) American actress

❧

When women go wrong,
men go right after them.

— *Mae West*
(1892-1980) American actress

❧

God help the man
who won't marry until he finds a perfect woman,
and God help him still more if he finds her.

— *Benjamin Tillett*

❧

Thank heaven.
A bachelor's life is no life
for a single man.

— *Samuel Goldwyn*
*(1879-1974) Warsaw-born, American film producer
when told his son was getting married*

❧

This fate is the newly married sir's.
To think she's his and find he's hers.
— *S. H. Dewhurst*

❧

It is always incomprehensible to a man that a woman
should ever refuse an offer of marriage.
— *Jane Austen*
(1775–1817) English writer

❧

A man'll seem like a person to a woman,
year in, year out.
She'll put up and she'll put up.
Then one day he'll do something maybe no worse
than what he's been a-doing all his life.
She'll look at him. And without no warning
he'll look like a varmint.
— *Marjorie Kinnan Rawlings*

❧

A man is never so weak
as when a woman is telling him how strong he is.
— *anonymous*

ટ

I insist on believing that some men are my equals.
— *Brigid Brophy*

ટ

Women have many faults, men have only two;
everything they say
and everything they do.
— *anonymous*

ટ

Macho does not prove mucho.
— *Zsa Zsa Gabor*
Hungarian actress

ટ

Probably the only place where a man
can feel really secure
is a maximum security prison,
except for the imminent threat of release.
— *Germaine Greer*

ટ

If men could get pregnant,
abortion would be a sacrament.
— *Florynce Kennedy*

❧

Men fantasize about being in bed with two women.
Women fantasize about it too because at least they'll
have someone to talk to when he falls asleep.
— *anonymous*

❧

Man—a creature made at the end of the week's work
when God was tired.
— *Mark Twain*
(1834-1910) American novelist

❧

MAN: an animal (whose)...chief occupation is
extermination of other animals and his own species,
which, however, multiplies with such insistent
rapidity as to infest the whole habitable
earth and Canada.
— *Ambrose Bierce*
(1842-1914) American satirist

❧

Here's to the happy man:
All the world loves a lover.
— *Ralph Waldo Emerson*
(1803-1882) American writer

❦

I like men to behave like men—strong and childish.
— *Françoise Sagan*

❦

No man thinks there is much ado about nothing
when the ado is about himself.
— *Anthony Trollope*
(1815-1882) English novelist

❦

My brain? It's my second favorite organ.
— *Woody Allen*
(1935-) American actor/writer

❦

Most of us grow up to be the kind of man
our mother's warned us against.
— *Brendan Behan*

❦

A man is like a phonograph with half a dozen
records. You soon get tired of them all,
and yet you have to sit at the table
whilst he reels them off to every new visitor.
— *George Bernard Shaw*
(1856-1950) Irish dramatist

ઢ

Behind every great man
there is a surprised woman.
— *Maryon Pearson*

ઢ

The follies which a man regrets most in his life
are those which he didn't commit
when he had the opportunity.
— *Helen Rowland*

ઢ

Men are creatures with two legs and eight hands.
— *Jayne Mansfield*
(1933-1967) American actress

ઢ

A woman may race to get a man a gift,
but it always ends in a tie.
— *Earl Wilson*

ઢ

Men of few words are the best men.
— *William Shakespeare*
(1564-1616) English writer

&

If you catch a man, throw him back.
— *Women's Liberation Slogan*

&

It is true that all married men have their own way,
but the trouble is
they don't all have their own way of having it!
— *Artemus Ward*
(1834–1867) American humorist

&

Can you imagine a world without men?
No crime, and lots of happy, fat women.
— *Nicole Hollander*

&

A man in the house is worth two in the street.
— *Mae West*
(1892–1980) American actress

&

Every man is as God hath made him,
and sometimes a great deal worse.
— *Miguel de Cervantes*
(1547–1616) Spanish novelist/poet
Don Quixote

❧

I only like two kinds of men: domestic and foreign.
— *Mae West*
(1892-1980) American actress

❧

God made some men big and others small.
Samuel Colt made all men equal.
— *John Thompson*

❧

He could have made many women happy
by remaining a bachelor.
He could also have made one woman happy
by remaining a bachelor.

— *anonymous*

❧

His mother should have thrown him away
and kept the stork.
— *Mae West*
(1892-1980) American actress

❧

A man is so in the way in the house.
— *Elizabeth Cleghorn Gaskell*
(1810-1865) English writer

Marriage

&

All marriages are happy.
It's living together afterwards that is difficult.
— *anonymous*

&

The web (of marriage) is fashioned of love. Yes, but
many kinds of love: romantic love first, then slow-
growing devotion, and playing through these, a
constantly rippling relationship. It is made a loyalties
and interdependencies and shared experiences. It is
woven of memories of meetings and conflicts; of
triumphs and disappointments. It is a web of
communication, a common language, and the
acceptance of lack of language, too.
— *Anne Morrow Lindbergh*
(1906-) American writer/aviator

&

In marriage vows, obey it you want to; but I should
think it would be more reasonable to have each one
promise to try to be worthy of love and honor; that
would at least be something one could work for.
— *Ruth Stout*

કે

Marriage is a romance in which
the hero dies in the first chapter.
— *anonymous*

કે

The world has suffered more from the ravages
of ill-advised marriages than from virginity.
— *Ambrose Bierce*
(1842-1914) American satirist

કે

A good marriage is like a casserole,
only those responsible for it
really know what goes in it.
— *anonymous*

કે

For a male and female to live
continuously together is...
biologically speaking,
an extremely unnatural condition.
— *Robert Briffault*

ॐ

Love matches are made by people who are content,
for a month of honey,
to condemn themselves to a life of vinegar.
— *Countess of Blessington*

ॐ

Marriage is like a hot bath.
Once you get used to it, it's not so hot.
— *anonymous*

ॐ

Marriage is like a box of chocolates.
You have to squeeze a few bottoms
to make sure you like what you are getting.
— *anonymous*

ॐ

Marry in haste;
repent at your leisure.
— *William Congreve*
(1670-1729) English dramatist

ॐ

Marriage is bliss. Ignorance is bliss. Ergo...
— *anonymous*

❧

A woman needs another point of view—
she should marry.
— *Bertha Reeder*

❧

Marry...into a family that will enable your children
to feel proud of both sides of the house.
— *Robert E. Lee*
(1807-1870) American military general

❧

A good marriage—
which means a continually improving marriage—
is a spiritual experience,
not a kind of glandular fever.
— *Virginia Baldwin*

❧

Winning a love is not enough.
Keep rewinning it...
In the last analysis,
it's up to you to save your marriage.
— *Hubert S. Howe*

ぞ◆

The most happy marriage
I can imagine to myself
would be the union
of a deaf man
to a blind woman.
— *Samuel Taylor Coleridge*
(1772-1834) English poet/critic

ぞ◆

Marriage is an adventure, like going to war.
— *Gilbert Keith Chesterton*
(1874-1936) English novelist/essayist

ぞ◆

The sum which two married people owe to one
another defies calculation. It is an infinite debt, which
can only be discharged through all eternity.
— *Johann Wolfgang von Goethe*
(1749-1832) German poet/novelist
Elective Affinities

ぞ◆

Marriage is the most delightful of the impermanencies
of life.
— *Anthony Gilbert*

ॐ

A happy marriage is still
the greatest treasure within the gift of fortune.
— *Eden Phillpotts*
(1862-1960) English author

ॐ

Is it better for a woman to marry a man
who loves her than a man she loves.
— *anonymous*

ॐ

The real marriage of true minds is
for any two people to possess a sense of humor
or irony pitched in exactly the same key,
so that their joint glances on any subject
cross like interarching searchlights.
— *Edith Wharton*
(1862-1937) American writer

ॐ

Newlyweds! In all your discovered differences,
think about your alikeness, imperfection,
and the right to personal improvement.
— *Elaine Cannon*
American writer

ે♪

The best decision I ever made in all my life
was to marry my husband at the right time
and in the right place.
— *Virginia Cook Sanders*

ે♪

Marriage:
The best method ever devised
for becoming acquainted.
— *Arnold Glasow*

ે♪

Often the difference between
a successful marriage and a mediocre one
consists of leaving about
three or four things a day unsaid.
— *Harlan Miller*

ે♪

Sometimes it was worth all the disadvantages
of marriage just to have that:
one friend in an indifferent world.
— *Erica Jong*
(1942-) American writer

❧

It comes as a great surprise to younger people that a
husband and wife must work at marriage all the years
of their life.
— *Dr. May E. Markewich*

❧

Neither is the man without the woman,
neither the woman without the man,
in the Lord.
— *I Corinthians 11:11*

❧

Marriage is a fine and sacred thing
if you make it so.
— *William Lyon Phelps*
(1865-1943) American scholar/educator

❧

Marriage requires the giving
and keeping of confidences,
the sharing of thoughts and feelings,
unfailing respect and understanding,
and a frank and gentle communication.
— *Richard L. Evans*

❧

The best goal is the success
of the marriage itself.
— *Dr. Paul W. Popenoe*

❧

For this cause shall a man
leave his father and mother, and cleave to his wife;
And they twain shall be one flesh:...
What therefore God hath joined together,
let not man put asunder.
— *Mark 10:6-9*

❧

One of my students wrote me
announcing his engagement.
"This is not going to be much of a wedding," he said,
"but it is going to be a wonderful marriage."
— *William Lyon Phelps*
(1865-1943) American scholar/educator

❧

A truly happy marriage is one in which a woman
gives the best years of her life
to the man who made them the best.
— *unknown*

❧

Marriage is the only war
in which you sleep with the enemy.

— *anonymous*

❧

Marriage is an empty box. It remains empty unless
you put in more than you take out.

— *unknown*

❧

Marriage is like a bank account.
You put it in, you take it out,
you lose interest.

— *Irwin Corey*

❧

Marriage is a matter of give and take,
but so far I haven't been able to find anybody
who'll take what I have to give.

— *Cass Daley*

❧

It is not good that man should be alone.

— *Genesis 2:18*

છે.

If you were paddling a canoe together, the important
thing is that each paddle in the same direction.
In marriage, if each has a different goal,
they will always be in trouble.
— *Dr. Paul W. Popenoe*

છે.

Marriage is popular because
it combines the maximum of temptation
with the maximum of opportunity.
— *George Bernard Shaw*
(1856-1950) Irish dramatist

છે.

It is a woman's business to get married
as soon as possible and
a man's to keep unmarried as long as he can.
— *George Bernard Shaw*
(1856-1950) Irish dramatist

છે.

A good wife and health
Are a man's best wealth.

— *unknown*

৵

There's a way of transferring funds
that is even faster than electronic banking.
It's called marriage.

— *James Holt*

৵

Marriage is a lottery
in which men stake their liberty
and women their happiness.

— *Madame de Rieux*

৵

The marriage of Marxism and feminism
has been like the marriage of husband and wife
depicted in English common law:
Marxism and feminism are one,
and that one is Marxism.

— *Heidi Hartmann*
The Unhappy Marriage of Marxism and Feminism

৵

Marriages are made in heaven
and consummated on Earth.

— *John Lyly*
(1554-1606) English novelist
Mother Bombie, 1590

If you want to sacrifice
the admiration of many men
for the criticism of one,
go ahead, get married.

— *Katharine Hepburn*
(1909-) American actress

Wedding is destiny,
and hanging likewise.

— *John Heywood*
(1497-1580) English dramatist poet

Marriage is a three ring circus:
engagement ring,
wedding ring,
and suffering.

— *anonymous*

I was married by a judge.
I should have asked for a jury.

— *Groucho Marx*
(1891-1977) comedian

৵

If it weren't for marriage,
men and women would have to fight
with total strangers.

— anonymous

৵

A good marriage would be between
a blind wife and a deaf husband.

— Michel Eyquem de Montaigne
(1533-1592) French writer/philosopher

৵

A good marriage is that in which each appoints
the other guardian of his solitude.

— Rainer Maria Rilke
(1875-1926) Austro-German poet

৵

Marriage isn't a word...
it's a sentence.

— King Vidor
(1928) The Crawl

❧

One cardinal rule of marriage
should never be forgotten:
"Give little, give seldom, and above all,
give grudgingly."
Otherwise, what could have been a proper marriage
could become an orgy of sexual lust.

— Ruth Smythers
Marriage advice for women

❧

The critical period in matrimony
is breakfast-time.

— Sir Alan Patrick Herbert
Uncommon Law

❧

To marry is to halve your rights
and double your duties.

— Arthur Schopenhauer
(1788–1860) German philosopher

❧

In olden times, sacrifices were made at the altar,
a practice which is still very much practiced.

— Helen Rowland

❧

There is no more lovely, friendly
and charming relationship,
communion or company
than a good marriage.
— *Martin Luther*
(1483-1546) German leader of Protestant Reformation
Table Talk

❧

The best part of married life is the fights.
The rest is merely so-so.
— *Thorton Wilder*
(1897-) American novelist
The Matchmaker, 1954

❧

Sexiness wears thin after a while and beauty fades,
but to be married to a man who makes you laugh
every day, ah, now that's a real treat!
— *Joanne Woodward*

❧

A happy marriage is a long conversation that always
seems too short.
— *André Maurois*
(1885-) French biographer/novelist

❧

Politics doesn't make strange bedfellows,
marriage does.

— *Groucho Marx*
(1891-1977) comedian

❧

Marriage is like a cage;
one sees the birds outside desperate to get in,
and those inside desperate to get out.

— *Michel Eyquem de Montaigne*
(1533-1592) French writer/philosopher

❧

Marriage is a great institution,
but I'm not ready for an institution.

— *Mae West*
(1892-1980) American actress

❧

Bigamy is having one wife too many.
Monogamy is the same.

— *Oscar Wilde*
(1854-1900) Irish poet/essayist

❧

May you always be happy,
and live at your ease;
Get a kind husband
And do as you please.

— *J.S. Ogilvie*

❧

Marriage is a lottery,
but you can't tear up your ticket
if you lose.

— *F. M. Knowles*

❧

Marriage is like a blind date.
Sometimes you just have to have
a little faith.

— *anonymous*

❧

Love is blind
and marriage is the institution
for the blind.

— *James Graham*

Marriage is the one subject on which
all women agree and all men disagree.
— *Oscar Wilde*
(1854–1900) Irish poet/essayist

It is the man and woman united
that makes the complete human being.
Separate she lacks his force
of body and strength of reason;
he her softness, sensibility and acute discernment.
Together they are most likely
to succeed in the world.
— *Benjamin Franklin*
(1706–1790) American scientist/statesman

Marriage is our last, best chance to grow up.
— *Joseph Barth*

The long-term accommodation that protects marriage
and other such relationships is...forgetfulness.
— *Alice Walker*

❧

Remember that if you ever put your marital problems
on the backburner,
they are sure to boil over.
— *anonymous*

❧

My most brilliant achievement was my ability
to be able to persuade my wife to marry me.
— *Sir Winston Churchill*
(1874-1965) English prime minister

❧

Marriage is a mistake every man should make.
— *George Jessel*

❧

Happy marriages begin
when we marry the one we love,
and they blossom when we love
the one we married.
— *Sam Levenson*

વ્ર

I will tell you the real secret of how to stay married.
Keep the cave clean.
They want the cave clean and spotless.
Air-conditioned, if possible.
Sharpen his spear, and stick it in his hand
when he goes out in the morning to spear that bear;
and when the bear chases him,
console him when he comes home at night,
and tell him what a big man he is,
and then hide the spear so he doesn't fall over it
and stab himself...
— *Jerome Chodorov & Joseph Fields*

વ્ર

Keep your eyes wide open before marriage,
half shut afterwards.
— *Benjamin Franklin*
(1706-1790) American scientist/statesman

વ્ર

Marriage is an attempt to turn a night owl
into a homing pigeon.
— *unknown*

❧

There is a fantasy that you fall in love,
get married and everything will automatically
be all right.
But in reality, falling in love is like a
vacation on a Caribbean island.
Marriage, on the other hand,
is like scratching a living from the steep,
stony slopes of Sicily.
They are two separate events.
— *David Birney*

❧

Marriage is a meal
where the soup is better than the dessert.
— *Austin O'Malley*

❧

Marriage is like life in this—
that it is a field of battle, and not a bed of roses.
— *Robert Louis Stevenson*
(1850-1894) Scottish poet/novelist

ॐ

People with ungovernable tempers
should never marry;
people who can't accept reality
should never marry;
people who don't enjoy responsibility
should never marry.
In fact, an awful lot of people
should never marry.

— Olivia de Havilland

ॐ

As told to a new bride by her father:
"Your marriage will be perfect when the rocks in
your husband's head fill the holes in yours."

— anonymous

ॐ

Marriage is the alliance of two people,
one of whom never remembers birthdays
and the other who never forgets.

— Ogden Nash
(1902–) American humorous poet

ॐ

Memories of a 90-year-old grandmother of the
three most important phrases her husband ever
said to her,
"I love you",
"you are so beautiful,"
and, "please forgive me."

— anonymous

ॐ

Marriage is not just spiritual communion and
passionate embraces; marriage is also three-meals-
a-day and remembering to carry out the trash.

— Dr. Joyce Brothers
American psychologist

ॐ

Two such as you with such a master speed
Cannot be parted nor be swept away
From one another once you are agreed
That life is only life forevermore
Together wing to wing and oar to oar.

— Robert Frost
(1874–1963) American poet

❧

Seek a happy marriage with wholeness of heart,
but do not expect to reach the promised land
without going through
some wilderness together.
— *Charlie W. Shedd*

❧

Marriage may have turned into a junk bond.
But nothing is so romantic as a risk.
— *Tracy Young*

❧

Marriage is not so much finding the right person
as it is being the right person.
— *anonymous*

❧

Marriage is three parts love
and seven parts forgiveness.
— *Langdon Mitchell*

❧

Marriage is not a ceremony! It is a creation!
— *Charlie W. Shedd*

❧

My wish for you is that you will marry someone
who is so great that it will take a whole
lifetime to know everything about him (her).
— *Charlie W. Shedd*

❧

It is a lovely thing to have a husband and wife
developing together.
That is what marriage really means;
helping one another to reach the full
status of being persons,
responsible and autonomous beings
who do not run away from life.
— *Paul Tournier*

❧

The great secret of a successful marriage is
to treat all disasters as incidents
and none of the incidents as disasters.
— *Harold Nicholson*

❧

Marriage is a fan club with only two fans.
— *Adrian Henri*

❧

On togetherness in marriage:
It must include
whatever amount of apartness
is right for each of you.
And if you allow plenty of room
for the "apartness" this has a way of
magnetizing the "togetherness."
— *Charlie W. Shedd*

❧

Marriage is that relationship
between man and woman
in which the independence is equal,
the dependence mutual
and the obligation reciprocal.
— *Louis Kaufman Anspacher*

❧

Marriage is too important
to be treated like a love affair.
— *Katharine Whitehorn*

❧

You will truly know you are married
when the bills start to come and
you learn to share the toothpaste.
— *Bernice Smith*

❧

A marriage between mature people is not an
escape but a commitment shared by two people
that becomes part of their commitment to
themselves and society.
— *Betty Friedan*

❧

More marriages might survive
if the partners realized that sometimes
the better comes after the worse.
— *Doug Larson*

❧

If marriage is to be a success, one should
obviously begin by marrying the right person.
— *Count Hermann Alexander Keyserling*
(1880-1946) German philosopher

❧

Marriage is the greatest educational
institution on earth.
— *Channing Pollock*

❧

A successful marriage requires falling in love
many times, always with the same person.
— *Mignon McLaughlin*

❧

It doesn't much signify whom one marries,
for one is sure to find out next morning
it was someone else.
— *Will Rogers*
(1879-1935) American humorist

❧

Marriage is a wonderful institution,
but who wants to live in an institution?
— *Groucho Marx*
(1891-1977) comedian

❧

Ah Mozart!
He was happily married—but his wife wasn't.
— *Victor Borge*

If you are afraid of loneliness,
don't marry.
— *Anton Chekhov*
(1860-1904) Russian dramatist/author

In matrimony,
to hesitate is sometimes to be saved.
— *Samuel Butler*
(1835-1902) English novelist

What's the definition of a tragedy?
Marrying a man for love and then
discovering he has no money.
— *anonymous*

Marriage is a lot like the Army,
everyone complains,
but you'd be surprised
at the large number that reenlist.
— *unknown*

੨੦

To me,
marriage essentially is a contract,
and there are so many loopholes in it.
— *Warren Beatty*
American actor

੨੦

Love is an obsessive delusion
that is cured by marriage.
— *Dr. Karl Bowman*

੨੦

We stay together,
but we distrust each other.
Ah, yes...
but isn't that the definition
of marriage?
— *Malcolm Bradbury*

੨੦

The deed involves sacrifice and risk.
— *Martin Buber*
(1878-) Jewish philosopher

ॐ

All tragedies are finished by death;
all comedies are ended by a marriage.
— *Lord Byron*
(1788-1824) English poet

ॐ

It was very good of God to let Carlyle and Mrs.
Carlyle marry one another and so make only two
people miserable instead of four.
— *Samuel Butler*
(1835-1902) English novelist

ॐ

My wife and I tried two or three times in the last
forty years to have breakfast together, but it was so
disagreeable we had to stop.
— *Sir Winston Churchill*
(1874-1965) English prime minister

ॐ

Marriage is a feast where the grace
is sometimes better than the dinner.
— *Charles Caleb Colton*

❧

Courtship to marriage is
as a very witty prologue to a very dull play.
— *William Congreve*
(1670-1729) English dramatist

❧

The dread of loneliness is greater
than the fear of bondage,
so we get married.
— *Cyril Connolly*

❧

There were three of us in the marriage,
so it was a bit crowded.
— *Diana, Princess of Wales*

❧

Winston, if I were married to you
I'd put poison in your coffee.
— *Lady Nancy Astor*
(1879-1964) English politician
to Sir Winston Churchill
(1874-1965) English prime minister

Nancy, if you were my wife, I'd drink it.
— *Sir Winston Churchill*
(in response)

🐌

I always thought that every woman should marry,
and no man.

— *Benjamin Disraeli*
(1804-1881) English statesman/author

🐌

There's only one way to have a happy marriage,
and as soon as I learn what it is
I'll get married again.

— *Clint Eastwood*
American actor

🐌

People change after they're married.
They die and become so very bourgeois.

— *Jane Fonda*
(1937-) American actress

🐌

When a woman gets married it is like jumping into a
hole in the ice in the middle of winter;
you do it once
and you remember it the rest of your days.

— *Maxim Gorky*
(1868-1936) Russian novelist

🐚

Most marriages don't add two people together,
they subtract one from the other.
— *Ian Fleming*
writer

🐚

I...chose my wife, as she did her wedding gown,
not for a fine glossy surface,
but such qualities as would wear well.
— *Oliver Goldsmith*
(1730-1774) Irish poet/novelist

🐚

We want playmates we own.
— *Jules Feiffer*

🐚

It's bloody impractical: to love, honor and obey.
If it weren't, you wouldn't have to sign a contract.
— *Katherine Hepburn*
(1909-) American actress

🐚

If you want to read about love and marriage
you've got to buy two separate books.
— *Alan King*

❧

Marriage is the process whereby
love ripens into vengeance.
— *Rudyard Kipling*
(1865-1936) English poet/writer

❧

The music at a wedding procession always reminds
me of the music of soldiers going into battle.
— *Heinrich Heine*
(1797-1856) German Jewish poet

❧

The husband who wants a happy marriage
should learn to keep his mouth shut
and his checkbook open.
— *Groucho Marx*
(1891-1977) comedian

❧

Couples are wholes and not wholes, what agrees
disagrees, the concordant is discordant. From all
things one and from one all things.
— *Heraclitus of Ephesus*
(500 BC) Greek philosopher

The surest way to be alone is to get married.
— *Gloria Steinem*
women's activist

'Tis more blessed to give than to receive;
for example, wedding presents.
— *Henry Louis Mencken*
(1880-1956) American editor

Our marriage works because
we each carry clubs of equal weight and size.
— *Paul Newman*
(1925-) American actor

Marriage is like paying an endless visit
in your worst clothes.
— *John Boynton Priestley*
(1894-1984) English novelist

Trust your husband, adore your husband,
and get as much as you can in your own name.
— *Joan Rivers*
(1933-) American entertainer

🙿

Marriage may often be a stormy lake, but celibacy
is almost always a muddy horsepond.
— *Thomas Love Peacock*
(1785-1866) English author

🙿

The only really happy folk are
married women and single men.
— *Henry Louis Mencken*
(1880-1956) American editor

🙿

The trouble with wedlock is
there's not enough wed and too much lock.
— *Christopher Morley*

🙿

Marriage is a friendship
recognized by the police.
— *Robert Louis Stevenson*
(1850-1894) Scottish poet/novelist

🙿

Matrimony—the high sea for which
no compass has yet been invented.
— *Heinrich Heine*
(1797-1856) German Jewish poet

❧

Heaven will be no heaven to me
if I do not meet my wife there.

— *Andrew Jackson*
(1767-1845) 7th American president

❧

Polygamy—how much more poetic it is to marry one
and love many.

— *Oscar Wilde*
(1854-1900) Irish poet/essayist

❧

Why does a woman work ten years to change
a man's habits and then complain that he's not
the man she married.

— *Barbra Streisand*
(1942-) singer/actress

❧

The proper basis for marriage is mutual
misunderstanding.

— *Oscar Wilde*
(1854-1900) Irish poet/essayist

ॐ

Advice to persons about to marry—
don't.

— *character, Punch*

ॐ

What delight we married people have to see these
poor fools decoyed into our condition.

— *Samuel Pepys*
(1633-1703) English diarist

ॐ

There is one thing worse than an absolutely
loveless marriage.
A marriage in which there is love,
but on one side only.

— *Oscar Wilde*
(1854-1900) Irish poet/essayist

ॐ

Marriage is based on the theory that when a man
discovers a particular brand of beer exactly to his
taste, he should at once throw up his job
and go to work at the brewery.

— *George Jean Nathan*
(1882-1958) American critic/author

꿩

Behold, I have set before you an open door,
and no man shall close it.
— *Revelation 3:8*

꿩

Oh! How many torments lie
in the small circle of a wedding ring!
— *Colley Cibber*
(1671-1757) *English dramatist/poet*

꿩

There are six requisites in every happy marriage. The
first is Faith and the remaining five are Confidence.
— *Elbert Hubbard*

꿩

If it were not for the presents,
an elopement would be preferable.
— *George Ade*
(1866-1944) *American author*

꿩

The crossing of the threshold is the first step into
the sacred zone of the universal source.
— *Joseph Campbell*

❧

We're too old to be single.
Why shouldn't we both be married instead
of sitting through the long winter evenings by our
solitary firesides?
Why shouldn't we make one fireside of it?
Come, let's be a comfortable couple and take care of
each other!
How glad we shall be, that we have somebody we
are fond of always, to talk to and sit with.
Let's be a comfortable couple. Now do, my dear!

— *Charles Dickens*
(1812-1870) English writer

❧

A sound marriage is not based
on complete frankness;
it is based
on a sensible reticence.

— *Morris L. Ernst*

❧

A happy marriage is the union of two forgivers.

— *Ruth Bell Graham*

❧

Original human nature
was not like the present but different.
The sexes were not two as they are now
but originally three in number;
there was man, woman and the union of the two...
the man was originally the child of the sun,
the woman of the earth,
and the man-woman of the moon,
which is made up of sun and earth...
[Now] when one of them meets his other half,
the actual half of himself,
the pair are lost in amazement of love
and friendship and intimacy...
these are the people who pass
their whole lives together...
The reason is that human nature was originally one
and we were a whole, and the desire and pursuit
of the whole is called love...

— Plato

(429-347 BC) Greek philosopher
referring to the teachings of Aristophanes

❧

...he's more myself than I am.
Whatever our souls are made of,
his and mine are the same...
If all else perished and he remained,
I should still continue to be,
and if all else remained and he were annihilated,
the universe would turn to be a might stranger...
He's always, always in my mind;
not as a pleasure to myself, but as my own being.

— Emily Brontë
(1818-1848) English writer
Wuthering Heights

❧

Those who have made unhappy marriages
walk on stilts,
while the happy ones are on a level with the crowd.
No one sees 'em.

— John Oliver Hobbes

❧

Take each other for better or worse
but not for granted.

— Arlene Dahl

&

Camerado, I give you my hand!
I give you my love more precious than money,
I give you myself before preaching or law;
Will you give me yourself?
Will you come travel with me?
Shall we stick by each other as long as we live?

— *Walt Whitman*
(1819-1892) American poet

&

A good relationship has a pattern like a dance
and is built on some of the same rules.
The partners do not need to hold on tightly,
because they move confidently in the same pattern,
intricate but gay and swift and free,
like a country dance of Mozart's.
To touch heavily would be to
arrest the pattern and freeze the moment,
to check the endlessly
changing beauty of its unfolding...
The joy of such a pattern is not only the joy of
creation or the joy of participation, it is
also the joy of living in the moment.

— *Anne Morrow Lindbergh*
(1906-) American writer/aviator

❧

Why the ring finger was chosen:
When the human body is cut open as the Egyptians
do and when dissections...are practiced on it, a very
delicate nerve is found which starts from the ring
finger and travels to the heart.
It is therefore, thought seemly to give to this finger in
preference to all others the honor of the ring, on
account of the loose connection which links it with
the principal organ.
— *Aulus Gellius*
(2nd century AD) Roman essayist

❧

A good marriage is at least 80 percent good luck
in finding the right person at the right time.
The rest is trust.
— *Nanette Newman*
English actress

❧

The first duty of love is to listen.
— *Paul Johannes Tillich*
(1886–) German-American theologian

❧

I belong to Bridegrooms anonymous.
Whenever I feel like getting married,
they send over a lady in a housecoat
and hair curlers to burn my toast for me.

— *Dick Martin*
(1923-) American comedian

❧

I am convinced there are not many marriages such as
ours. I suppose every bride thinks so. But my belief
is based in something more than love for my
husband. I have seen much of married people, and I
have known much of marriage, but I have never
known any union so sweet, and beautiful, so spiritual
and soul-satisfying as ours. I swell in sunshine and
my heart sings with happiness.

— *Lella Secor*

❧

The people who enjoy marriage
are those who first have learned to live life itself.
You can't create intimacy without identity.

— *Richard Rohr*

❧

The union of husband and wife
in heart, body and mind is intended by God
for their mutual joy;
for the help and comfort given one another
in prosperity and adversity; and,
when it is God's will,
for the procreation of children and
their nurture in the knowledge
and love of the Lord.
Therefore marriage is not to be
entered into unadvisedly or
lightly, but reverently, deliberately,
and in accordance with
the purposes for which it was instituted by God.
— *The Celebration and Blessing of a Marriage*
The Book of Common Prayer (Episcopal)

❧

Marriage has many pains,
but celibacy has no pleasures.
— *anonymous*

I consider everybody as having a right to
marry once in their lives for love.

— *Jane Austen*
(1775-1817) English writer

Marriage is the union of two divinities that
a third might be born on earth.
It is the union of two souls in a strong love
for the abolishment of separateness.
It is that higher unity which fuse
the separate unities within the two spirits.
It is the golden ring within a chain
whose beginning is a glance,
and whose ending is Eternity.
It is the pure rain that falls
from an unblemished sky
to fructify and bless the fields of divine Nature.

— *Kahlil Gibran*
(1883-1931) Lebanonese poet/philosopher

Marriage should be a duet—
when one sings, the other claps.

— *Joe Murray*

We have taken the seven steps.
You have become mine forever.
Yes, we have become partners.
I have become yours.
Hereafter, I cannot live without you.
Do not live without me.
Let us share the joys.
We are word and meaning, united.
You are thought and I am sound.
May the nights be honey-sweet for us;
may the mornings be honey-sweet for us;
may the earth be honey-sweet for us;
may the heavens be honey-sweet for us.
May the plants be honey-sweet for us;
may the sun be all honey for us;
may the cows yield us honey-sweet milk!
As the heavens are stable,
as the earth is stable,
as the mountains are stable,
as the whole universe is stable,
so may our union be permanently settled.

— *Hindu marriage ritual*
Seven Steps

Be thou magnified,
O bridegroom, like Abraham,
and blessed like Isaac,
and increase like Jacob,
walking in peace and living in righteousness...
And thou,
O bride, be magnified like Sarah,
and rejoice like Rebecca,
and increase like Rachel,
being glad in peace and living
and keeping the bounds of the law...
— *Greek Orthodox marriage service*

What counts in making a happy marriage
is not so much how compatible you are,
but how you deal with incompatibility.
— *George Levinger*

Molehills are mountains
when you are first married.
— *Kathleen Norris*
(1880-) American novelist

❧

Let me insist that fidelity in marriage
cannot be merely that negative attitude
so frequently imagined; it must be active.
To be content not to deceive one's
wife or husband would be an indication of indigence,
not one of love.
Fidelity demands far more:
it wants the good of the beloved,
and when it acts in behalf of that good
it is creating in its own presence the neighborhood...
Thus as persons
a married couple are a mutual creation,
and to become persons is the double achievement
of "active love."

— *Denis de Rougemont*
Love in the Western World

❧

MARRIAGE, n. a community consisting of a master,
a mistress, and two slaves, making in all, two.

— *Ambrose Bierce*
(1842-1914) American satirist
The Devil's Dictionary, 1906

❧

Take a lump of wet clay, wet it, pat it,
And make an image of me, and an image of you.
Then smash them, crash them, and add a little water.
Break them and remake them into an image of you
And an image of me.
Then in my clay, there's a little of you.
And in your clay, there's a little of me.
And nothing ever shall us sever;
Living, we'll sleep in the same quilt,
And dead, we'll be buried together.

— *Madame Kuan*

❧

What greater thing is there
for two human souls
than to feel
that they are joined...
to strengthen each other...
to be at one
with each other in silent
unspeakable memories.

— *George Eliot*
(1819-1880) English writer

❧

...marriage seems to me a subjectivist fiction with two
points of view often deeply in conflict, sometimes
fortuitously congruent.
Marriages go bad not when love fades—
love can modulate into affection
without driving two people apart—
but when this understanding about
the balance of power breaks down.

— *Phyllis Rose*
Parallel Views: Five Victorian Marriages

❧

This we know, all things are connected,
like the blood which unites one family.
All things are connected.
Whatever befalls the earth,
befalls the sons of the earth.
Man did not weave the web of life;
he is merely a strand in it.
Whatever he does to the web,
he does to himself.

— *Chief Seattle*
Dwamish Tribe

The essence of a good marriage
is respect for each other's personality
combined with that deep intimacy,
physical, mental and spiritual,
which makes a serious love
between man and woman
the most fructifying of all human experiences.
Such love, like everything that is great and precious,
demands its own morality,
and frequently entails a sacrifice
of the less to the greater;
but such sacrifice must be voluntary,
for, where it is not,
it will destroy the very basis of the love
for the sake of which it is made.

— *Bertrand Russell*
(1872-1970) English philosopher
Marriage and Morals

There are two tests in a happy marriage—
riches and poverty.

— *anonymous*

Music

ᔕᕈ

If music be the food of love,
     play on.
— *William Shakespeare*
(1564-1616) English writer

ᔕᕈ

Let every man sing his own song in life.
— *John A. Widtsoe*

ᔕᕈ

When hearts listen, angels sing.
— *unknown*

ᔕᕈ

I loved you first: but afterwards your love,
outsoaring mine, sang such a loftier song.
— *Christina Rossetti*
(1830-1894) English poet

ᔕᕈ

Music is love in search of a word.
— *Sidney Lanier*
(1842-1881) American poet

She is the heart that strikes a whole octave.
After her, all songs are possible.

— *Rainer Maria Rilke*
(1875-1926) Austro-German poet

O, my luve is like a red, red rose.
That's newly sprung in June:
O, my luve is like the melodie
That's sweetly played in tune.

— *Robert Burns*
(1759-1796) Scottish poet

Love is like a violin.
The music may stop now and then,
but the strings remain forever.

— *Bacher*

Music I heard with you
was more than music;
and bread I broke with you
was more than bread.

— *unknown*

Passion

❧

My bounty is as boundless as the sea,
my love as deep;
the more I give to thee,
the more I have,
for both are infinite.

— *William Shakespeare*
(1564-1616) English writer

❧

Anyone can be passionate,
but it takes real lovers to be silly.

— *Rose Franken*

❧

In endowing us with memory,
nature has revealed to us a truth
utterly unimaginable to the unreflective creation,
the truth of immortality....
The most ideal human passion is love,
which is also the most absolute and animal
and one of the most ephemeral.

— *George Santayana*
(1865-1952) Spanish philosopher
Reason in Religion

ॐ

This is one of the miracles of love:
It gives...a power of seeing through its own
enchantments and yet not being disenchanted.

— *C. S. Lewis*
(1898-) English author

ॐ

When a person that one loves is in the world
and alive and well...then to miss them is only a new
flavor, a salty sharpness in experience.

— *Winifred Holtby*

ॐ

To enlarge or illustrate
this power and effect of love
is to set a candle in the sun.

— *Robert Burton*

ॐ

Here are fruits, flowers, leaves and branches.
And here is my heart which beats only for you.

— *Paul Verlaine*
(1844-1896) French poet

❧

God is Love—I dare say.
But what a mischievous devil Love is!
— *Samuel Butler*
(1835-1902) English novelist

❧

A great flame follows a little spark.
— *Dante Alighieri*
The Divine Comedy

❧

Love, like Death,
Levels all ranks,
and lays the shepherd's crook
Beside the scepter.
— *Edward Bulwer-Lytton*
(1803-1873) English novelist/dramatist
The Lady of Lyons

❧

The lover who has not felt the hot tears
rise at the sight of some slight,
infinitely poignant imperfection
in the body of the beloved,
has never loved.
— *Mervyn Levy*

❧

I am Tarzan of the Apes.
I want you.
I am yours.
You are mine.
— *Edgar Rice Burroughs*
Tarzan of the Apes, 1914

❧

I gave what other women gave
That stepped out of their clothes,
But when this soul, its body off,
Naked to naked goes,
He it has found shall find therein
What none other knows.
— *William Butler Yeats*
(1865–1939) Irish poet
The Winding Stair and Other Poems

❧

Child, you are like a flower,
So sweet and pure and fair.
I look at you, and sadness
Touches me with a prayer.
— *Heinrich Heine*
(1797–1856) German Jewish poet

&❧

There are two things to aim at in life:
first, to get what you want; and,
after that, to enjoy it.
Only the wisest of mankind achieve the second.

— *Logan Pearsall Smith*
Afterthoughts, 1931

&❧

The month of May was come,
when every lusty heart beginneth to blossom,
and to bring forth fruit;
for like as herbs and trees
bring forth fruit and flourish in May,
in likewise every lusty heart
that is in any manner a lover,
springeth and flourisheth in lusty deeds.
For it giveth unto all lovers courage,
that lusty month of May.

— *Sir Thomas Malory*
(-1471) English prose writer

&❧

Love knows nothing of order.

— *St. Jerome*
(340-420 AD) Father/Doctor of Christian Church
Letter 7

❧

We never leave each other.
When does your mouth
say goodbye to your heart?
— *Mary TallMountain*

❧

Thou truly canst not guide whom thou lovest;
but God guideth whom He will;
and He best knoweth those who yield to guidance.
— *The Koran*
Chapter 28:55

❧

Our chief want in life is somebody
who shall make us do what we can.
— *Ralph Waldo Emerson*
(1803-1882) American writer
The Conduct of Life

❧

With each touch of you
I am fresh bread
warm and rising.

— *Pat Parker*

In everyone's life, at some time,
our inner fire goes out.
It is then burst into flame by an encounter
with another human being.
We should all be thankful for those people
who rekindle the inner spirit.

— *Albert Schweitzer*
(1875-1965) Alsatian theologian/medical missionary

For God's sake hold your tongue,
and let me love.

— *John Donne*
(1572-1631) English poet
The Canonization

I waited
For the phone to ring
And when at last
It didn't,
I knew it was you.

— *Eleanor Bron*

In peace, Love tunes the shepherd's reed;
In war, he mounts the warrior's steed;
In halls, in gay attire is seen;
In hamlets, dances on the green.
Love rules the court, the camp, the grove,
And men below, and saints above;
Is heaven, and heaven is love.

— *Sir Walter Scott*
(1771-1832) Scottish poet/novelist
The Lay of the Last Minstrel, 1805

Unrememberd and afar
I watched you as I watched a star,
Through darkness struggling into view
And I loved you better than you knew.

— *Elizabeth Akers Allen*

A fire that no longer blazes
is quickly smothered in ashes.
Only a love that scorches and dazzles
is worthy of the name.
Mine is like that.

Juliette Drouet

❧

Man and woman are two locked caskets,
of which each contains the key to the other.

— *Isak Dinesen*

(1885-1962) Danish writer
Winter Tales

❧

Man is the only animal that blushes.
Or needs to.

— *Mark Twain*

(1834-1910) American novelist

❧

Union gives strength.

— *Aesop*

(6th century BC) Greek author
The Bundle of Sticks

❧

I see only you, think only of you,
touch only you, breathe you, desire you,
dream of you; in a word, I love you!

— *Juliette Drouet*

❧

No human creature can give orders to love.
— *George Sand*
(1804-1876) French writer

❧

An orgasm a day keeps the doctor away.
— *Mae West*
(1892-1980) American actress

❧

Come live with me, and be my love,
And we will some new pleasures prove
Of golden sands, and crystal brooks,
With silken lines, and silver hooks.
— *John Donne*
(1572-1631) English poet
The Bait

❧

My love for you's so strong
That no one could kill it—
not even you.
— *Anna Akhmatova*
(1888-) Russian poet

ॐ

May the gods grant you all things
which your heart desires,
and may they give you a husband and a home
and gracious concord,
for there is nothing greater and better than this—
when a husband and wife
keep a household in oneness of mind,
a great woe to their enemies
and joy to their friends,
and win high renown.

— Homer
(before 700 BC) Greek author
The Odessey

ॐ

Absence diminishes mediocre passions
and increases great ones,
as the wind blows out candles
and fans fire.
— François, Duc de La Rochefoucauld
(1613-1680) French writer

❧

The fundamental error of their matrimonial union;
that of having based a permanent contract
on a temporary feeling.

— *Thomas Hardy*
(1840-1928) English novelist/poet
Juse the Obscure, 1895

❧

What is yours is mine,
and all mine is yours.

— *Titus Maccius Plautus*
(254-184 BC) Roman comedy writer

❧

Sex is the biggest nothing of all time.

— *Andy Warhol*
(1926-1987) American painter

❧

Come live with me, and be my love;
And we will all the pleasures prove
That valleys, groves, hills, and fields,
Woods or steepy mountain yields.

— *Christopher Marlowe*
(1564-1593) English dramatist
The Passionate Shepherd to His Love, 1589

❧

You're obstinate, pliant, merry,
morose, all at once.
For me there's no living with you,
or without you.

— *Martial*

*(38-104 AD) Roman epigrammatist
Epigrams*

❧

I believe a little incompatibility
is the spice of life,
particularly if he has income
and she is pattable.

— *Ogden Nash*

(1902-) American humorous poet

❧

Those that love the most speak least.
— *George Pettie*

❧

There is no question for which
you are not the answer.
— *Bonnie Zucker Goldsmith*

❧

So we grew together,
Like to a double cherry,
seeming parted,
But yet an union in partition;
Two lovely berries molded on one stem.

— *William Shakespeare*
(1564-1616) English writer
A Midsummer-Night's Dream

❧

Let all thy joys be as the month of May,
And all thy days be as a marriage day:
Let sorrow, sickness, and a troubled mind
Be stranger to thee.

— *Francis Quarles*
(1592-1644) English poet
To a Bride

❧

Men are April when they woo,
December when they wed:
maids are May when they are maids,
but the sky changes when they are wives.

— *William Shakespeare*
(1564-1616) English writer
As You Like It

ঌ

The union of hands and hearts.
— *Jeremy Taylor*
Sermons, 1653

ঌ

When two people are under the influence
of the most violent, most insane, most delusive,
and most transient of passions,
they are required to swear
that they will remain
in that excited, abnormal,
and exhausting condition
continuously until death do them part.
— *George Bernard Shaw*
(1856–1950) Irish dramatist
Getting Married

ঌ

To live happily with other people
one should ask of them
only what they can give.
— *Tristan Bernard*
(1866–1947) French dramatist
L'Enfant prodigue du Vesinet

Happy, thrice happy and more,
are they whom an unbroken bond unites
and whose love shall know no sundering quarrels
so long as they shall live.

— *Horace*
(65-8 BC) Roman poet

As one whom his mother comforteth,
so will I comfort you.

— *Isaiah 66:13*

Love—bittersweet, irrepressible—
loosens my limbs and I tremble.

— *Sappho*
(620-565 BC) Greek lyric poet

I have drunk of the wine of life at last,
I have known the thing best worth knowing,
I have been warmed through and through,
never to grow quite cold again till the end.

— *Edith Wharton*
(1862-1937) American writer

My fair one,
let us swear an eternal friendship.
— *Moliére*

(1622-1673) French playwright/actor
Le Bourgeois Gentilhomme, 1670

To me, fair friends, you never can be old,
For as you were when first your eye I ey'd,
Such seems your beauty still.
— *William Shakespeare*

(1564-1616) English writer

When one has once had
the good luck to love intensely,
life is spent in trying to recapture
that aurdor and that illumination.
— *Albert Camus*

(1913-1960) French novelist/essayist

Shall we make a new rule of life from tonight:
always to try to be a little kinder than is necessary?
— *Sir James M. Barrie*

(1860-1937) English dramatist/novelist
The Little White Bird, 1902

He first deceased;
She for a little tried
To live without him,
liked it not, and died.
— *Sir Henry Wooton*
(1568-1639) English poet/diplomat

Justice is the only worship.
Love is the only priest.
Ignorance is the only slavery.
Happiness is the only good.
The time to be happy is now,
The place to be happy is here,
The way to be happy is to make others so.
— *Robert Green Ingersoll*
(1833-1899) American lawyer/orator

I love you so passionately,
that I hide a great part of my love,
not to oppress you with it.
— *Marie de Rabutin-Chantal*

Man's best possession
is a sympathetic wife.

— *Euripides*
(485-406 BC) Greek tragic dramatist

Youth's the season made for joys,
Love is then our duty.

— *John Gay*
(1685-1732) English poet/playwright

Daisy, Daisy, give me your answer, do!
I'm half crazy, all for the love of you!
It won't be a stylish marriage,
I can't afford a carriage,
But you'll look sweet upon the seat
Of a bicycle built for two!

— *Harry Dacre*
Daisy Bell, 1892

The sight of you is good for sore eyes.

— *Jonathan Swift*
(1667-1745) English writer
Polite Conversation, 1738

❧

This is the hardest of all:
to close the open hand out of love,
and keep modest as a giver.
— *Friedrich W. Nietzsche*
(1844-1900) German philosopher

❧

Very little is needed
to make a happy life.
— *Marcus Aurelius*
Meditations

❧

In America sex is an obsession;
in other parts of the world it is a fact.
— *Marlene Dietrich*
(1901-1992) German actress

❧

Young love is a flame, often very hot and fierce
but still only light and flickering.
The love of the older and disciplined heart
is as coals deep-burning, unquenchable.
— *Henry Ward Beecher*

❧

When you kiss me,
jaguars lope through my knees;
when you kiss me,
my lips quiver like bronze violets;
oh, when you kiss me.
— *Diane Ackerman*

❧

Human thirsts are satisfied from time to time,
but the thirst of the human skin is never satisfied
so long as it lives.
— *Joyce Carol Oates*

❧

The great pairs of lovers in history
only became the great pairs of lovers in history
because they never got each other.
— *anonymous*

❧

How long I've loved thee,
and how well—I dare not tell!
— *Margaret Deland*
(1857-1945) American novelist

&

I felt your love as a benediction
In tranquil branches above me spread,
Over my sometimes troubled head.
— *Vita Sackville-West*

&

But there's nothing half so sweet in life
As love's young dream.
— ***Thomas Moore***
(1779-1852) *Irish poet*

&

The Bible contains six admonishments to
homosexuals and 362 admonishments to
heterosexuals. That doesn't mean that God
doesn't love heterosexuals. It's just that they need
more supervision.

— *Lynn Lavner*

&

We find rest in those we love,
and we provide a resting place in ourselves
for those who love us.
— ***St. Bernard of Clairvaux***
(1090-1153) *Christian saint*

The most exciting attractions
are between two opposites that never meet.
— *Andy Warhol*
(1926-1987) American painter

I have to find a girl attractive
or it's like trying to start a car
without an ignition key.
— *Jonathan Aitken*

It has to be admitted that
we English have sex on the brain,
which is a very unsatisfactory place to have it.
— *Malcolm Muggeridge*

There is a passion for hunting something deeply
implanted in the human breast.
— *Charles Dickens*
(1812-1870) English writer

❧

A kiss can be a comma, a question mark
or an exclamation point.
— *Mistinguette*

❧

Tenderness is greater proof of love
than the most passionate of vows.
— *Marlene Dietrich*
(1901-1992) German actress

❧

Compassion is the most necessary ingredient in all
relationships. Everything depends on it.
— *Jane Stanton Hitchcock*

❧

Their bodies were so close together that
there was no room for real affection.
— *Stanislaw J. Lec*

❧

Can I ever know you
Or you know me?
— *Sara Teasdale*
(1884-1933) American poet

Prudence

❧

He early on let her know who is the boss.
He looked her right in the eye and clearly said,
"You're the boss."

— anonymous

❧

Love is what happens to men and women
who don't know each other.
— William Somerset Maugham
(1874-) English writer

❧

A man who marries a woman to educate her
falls a victim to the same fallacy as
the woman who marries a man to reform him.
— Elbert Hubbard

❧

Those two fatal words,
Mine and Thine.
— Miguel de Cervantes
(1547-1616) Spanish novelist/poet

ᘓ

The perfect love affair is one
which is conducted entirely by post.

— *George Bernard Shaw*
(1856-1950) Irish dramatist

ᘓ

A lover tries to stand in well
with the pet dog of the house.

— *Moliére*
(1622-1673) French playwright/actor

ᘓ

The only thing that holds a marriage together is the
husband bein' big enough to keep his mouth shut, to
step back and see where his wife is wrong.

— *character, Archie Bunker*
All in the Family

ᘓ

To keep your marriage brimming,
With love in the loving cup,
Whenever you're wrong, admit it;
Whenever you're right, shut-up!

— *Ogden Nash*
(1902-   ) American humorous poet

Look before you leap,
For as you sow,
you're likely to reap.

— *Samuel Butler*
(1835-1902) English novelist

Remember always:
Arrows pierce the body,
but harsh words pierce the soul.

— *Spanish proverb*

There's one sad truth in life I've found
While journeying east to west.
The only folks we really wound
Are those we love the best.
We flatter those we scarcely know,
We please the fleeing guest.
And deal full many a thoughtless blow,
To those we love the best.

— *anonymous*

≽❧

Long engagements give people the opportunity of
finding out each other's character before marriage,
which is never advisable.

— *Oscar Wilde*
(1854-1900) Irish poet/essayist

≽❧

Eggs and vows
are easily broken.

— *Japanese proverb*

≽❧

How often a careless, unkind word
spoken can spoil your day, wreck some
big job or deal, hurt a loved one, lose a friend.
Many of us, through ignorance,
thoughtlessness, or want of judgement,
wound those whom we love best and
most wish to help.

— *Alfred A. Montapert*

≽❧

Obey the customs
Of the village you enter.

— *Japanese proverb*

ॐ

The mouth is the cause
of calamity.
— *Japanese proverb*

ॐ

Observe the prudent; they in silence sit,
Display no learning, and affect no wit;
They hazard nothing, nothing they assume,
But know the useful art of acting dumb.
— *George Crabbe*
(1754-1832) English poet

ॐ

Let there be spaces in your togetherness,
And let the ends of the heavens dance between you.
Love one another, but make not a bond of love...
Fill each other's cup but drink not from one cup.
— *Kahlil Gibran*
(1883-1931) Lebanonese poet/philosopher

ॐ

It's only in silence
that you can judge of your relationship to a person.
— *Dorothy M. Richardson*

Romance

❧

A lady's imagination is very rapid;
it jumps from admiration to love,
from love to matrimony in a moment.

— *Jane Austen*
(1775-1817) English writer
Pride and Prejudice

❧

For in my mind,
of all mankind
I love but you alone.

— *anonymous*

❧

Over the mountains and over the waves,
Under the fountains and under the graves;
Under floods that are deepest,
which Neptune obey,
Over rocks that are steepest,
Love will find out the way.

— *anonymous*

Wild Nights - Wild Nights!
Were I with thee
Wild Nights should be
Our luxury!

Futile - the Winds -
To a Heart in port -
Done with the Compass -
Done with the Chart!

Rowing in Eden -
Ah, the Sea!
Might I but moor - Tonight -
In Thee!

— Emily Dickinson
(1830-1886) American poet

Abstinence sows sand all over
The ruddy limbs and flaming hair,
But Desire Gratified
Plants fruits of life and beauty there.

— William Blake
(1757-1827) English poet/artist

❧

[Love] is the perfume of that wondrous flower,
the heart, and without that sacred passion,
that divine swoon, we are less than beasts,
but with it, earth is heaven,
and we are gods.
— *Robert Green Ingersoll*
(1833-1899) American lawyer/orator

❧

Two shall be born,
the whole wide world apart,
and speak in different tongues
and have no thought
each of the other's being and botice...
One day out of darkness they shall meet
and read life's meaning in each other's eyes.
— *Susan Marr Spalding*

❧

In real love
you want the other person's good.
In romantic love
you want the other person.
— *Margaret Anderson*

When you came you were like red wine and honey,
And the taste of you burnt my mouth
with its sweetness.
Now you are like morning bread,
Smooth and pleasant.
I hardly taste you at all,
for I know your savor;
But I am completely nourished.
— *Amy Lowell*
(1874-1925) American poet
A Decade

O when the world's at peace
and every man is free
then will I go down unto my love.
O and I may go down
several times before that.
— *Wendell Berry*
The Mad Farmer's Love Song

On life's vast ocean diversely we sail,
Reason the card, but Passion is the gale.
— *Alexander Pope*
(1688-1744) English poet

⁊⁊

Body of my woman,
I will live on through your marvelousness.
My thirst, my desire without end, my wavering road!
Dark river beds down which the eternal thirst is
flowing, and the fatigue is flowing,
and the grief without shore.

— *Pablo Neruda*

⁊⁊

...It is said by some that there is no fixed time
or order between the kiss and the pressing
or scratching with the nails or finger,
but that all these things should be done generally
before sexual union takes place,
while striking and making the various sounds
generally takes place at the time of the union.
Vatsyayana, however, thinks that anything
may take place at any time,
for love does not care for time or order...

— *The Kama Sutra of Vatsyayana*

⁊⁊

Keep me as the apple of the eye,
hide me under the shadow of thy wings.

— *Psalm 17:8*

❧

Breathless, we flung us on the windy hill,
Laughed in the sun,
and kissed the lovely grass.
— *Rupert Brooke*
The Hill, 1910

❧

Jacob served seven years for Rachel;
and they seemed unto him but a few days,
for the love he had to her.
— *Genesis 29:20*

❧

Pains of love be sweeter far
Than all other pleasures are.
— *John Dryden*
(1631–1700) English poet
Tyrannic Love

❧

It is with our passions,
as it is with fire and water,
they are good servants but bad masters.
— *Sir Roger L'Estrange*

❧

...because two bodies, naked and entwined,
leap over time, they are invulnerable,
nothing can touch them,
they return to the source,
there is no you, no I,
no tomorrow, no yesterday,
no names, the truth of two in a single body,
a single soul, oh total being...

— *Octavio Paz*
(1914-) Mexican poet/writer
Sunstone

❧

Give me that man that is not passion's slave,
And I will wear him in my heart's core, ay,
In my heart of hearts.

— *William Shakespeare*
(1564-1616) English writer

❧

Who can give law to lovers?
Love is a greater law to itself.

— *Anicius Manlius Severinus Boethius*
(480-524 AD) Roman philosopher/statesman

If the heart of a man is depress'd with cares,
The mist is dispelled when a woman appears.
— *John Gay*
(1685-1732) English poet/playwright
The Beggar's Opera, 1728

Thou art to me
a delicious torment.
— *Ralph Waldo Emerson*
(1803-1882) American writer

Never love unless you can
Bear with all the faults of man.
— *Thomas Campion*
(1567-1620) English poet/composer

So long as man remains free
he strives for nothing
so incessantly and so painfully
as to find someone to worship.
— *Fëdor Dostoevski*
(1821-1881) Russian author
The Brothers Karamazov, 1879

Escape me?
Never—
While I am I, and you are you.
— *Robert Browning*
(1812-1889) English poet
Life in a Love

I slept and dreamed that life was beauty.
I woke—and found that life was duty;
Was my dream, then, a shadowy lie?
Toil on, sad heart, courageously,
And thou shalt find thy dream shall be
A noonday light and truth to thee.
— *Ellen Sturgis Hooper*

Oh, hasten not this loving act,
Rapture where self and not-self meet:
My life has been the awaiting you,
Your footfall was my own heart's beat.
— *Paul Valéry*
(1871-1945) French poet

৯

I'd love to get you
On a slow boat to China.
All to myself alone.
— *Frank Loesser*
On a Slow Boat to China, 1948

৯

I could dispense with life sooner
than with your love.
— *Juliette Drouet*

৯

The meeting of two personalities
is like the contact of two chemical substances:
if there is an reaction,
both are transformed.
— *Carl Jung*
(1875-1961) Swiss psychiatrist
Modern Man in Search of a Soul, 1933

৯

On wings of song, my dearest, I will carry you off.
— *Heinrich Heine*
(1797-1856) German Jewish poet

❧

No riches from his scanty store
My lover could impart;
He gave a boon I valued more—
He gave me all his heart!
— *Helen Maria Williams*

❧

I shall love you in December
With the love I gave in May!
— *John Alexander Joyce*

❧

Love at the lips was touch
as sweet as I could bear;
And once that seemed too much;
I lived on air.

— *Robert Frost*
(1874–1963) American poet
To Earthward

❧

Habit, of which passion must be wary,
may all the same be the sweetest part of love.
— *Elizabeth Bowen*
(1899–) Anglo-Irish novelist

❧

I humbly do beseech you of your pardon
For too much loving you.
— *William Shakespeare*
(1564-1616) English writer
Othello

❧

Love consists in this,
that two solitudes protect
and touch and greet each other.
— *Rainer Maria Rilke*
(1875-1926) Austro-German poet
Letters to a Young Poet

❧

My true-love hath me heart, and I have his,
By just exchange one for the other given:
I hold his dear, and mine he cannot miss,
There never was a better bargain driven.
— *Sir Philip Sidney*

❧

I loved him for himself alone.
— *Richard Brinsley Sheridan*
(1751-1816) Irish dramatist

🐦

A kiss
is something which you cannot give
without taking,
and cannot take
without giving.

— *anonymous*

🐦

Love means
never having to say
you're sorry.

— *Erich Segal*
Love Story, 1970

🐦

I was a child and she was a child,
In this kingdom by the sea,
but we loved with a love that was more than love—
I and my Annabel Lee—
With a love that the winged seraphs of Heaven
Coveted her and me.

— *Edgar Allan Poe*
(1809-1849) American poet/short story writer
Annabel Lee, 1849

❧

Give all to love;
Obey thy heart;
Friends, kindred, days,
Estate, good fame,
Plans, credit and the Muse,
Nothing refuse.
— *Ralph Waldo Emerson*
(1803–1882) American writer

❧

I hope before long to crush
you in my arms
and cover you
with a million kisses
burning as though
beneath the equator.
— *Napoleon Bonaparte*
(1769–1821) French general/leader
to Josephine

❧

You are everything to me.
— *Sarah Bernhardt*
(1844–1923) French actress

❧

My love's
More richer than my tongue.
— *William Shakespeare*
(1564-1616) English writer
King Lear

❧

'Tis strange what a man may do,
and a woman yet think him an angel.
— *William Makepeace Thackeray*
(1811-1863) English novelist
Henry Esmond

❧

Lovers' quarrels are the renewal of love.
— *Terence*
(195-159 BC) Roman comic dramatist
Andria (The Lady of Andros)

❧

I arise from dreams of thee
In the first sweet sleep of night,
When the winds are breathing low,
And the stars are shining bright.
— *Percy Bysshe Shelley*
(1792-1822) English poet

ॐ

My lifetime listens to yours.
— *Muriel Rukeyser*

ॐ

In a great romance,
each person basically plays a part
that the other really likes.
— *Elizabeth Ashley*

ॐ

I wasn't kissing her,
I was whispering in her mouth.
— *Chico Marx*
(1886-1979) Marx Brothers/American film comedian

ॐ

Nothing spoils romance so much
as a sense of humor in the woman.
— *Oscar Wilde*
(1854-1900) Irish poet/essayist

❧

The world is so empty if one thinks only of
mountains, rivers and cities;
but to know someone here and there
who thinks and feels with us, and who,
though distant, is close to us in spirit,
this makes the earth for us an inhabited garden.
— *Johann Wolfgang van Goethe*
(1749-1832) German poet/novelist

❧

Being with you is like walking on a very clear
morning—definitely the sensation of belonging there.
— *E. B. White*
(1899-1985) humorist/writer

❧

If love be timid it is not true.
— *Spanish proverb*

❧

Love is a second life;
it grows into the soul, warms every vain,
and beats in every pulse.
— *Joseph Addison*
(1672-1719) English poet/essayist

❧

Nothing is more exciting
and bonding in relationships
than creating together.

— *Stephen Covey*
Motivational speaker

❧

We are crazy. People have said it.
We know it. Yet we go on.
But being crazy together is just fine.

— *Ray Bradbury*

❧

Things that are lovely tear my heart in two—
Moonlight on still pools, You.

— *Dorothy Dow*

❧

No love, no friendship
can cross the path of our destiny
without leaving some mark on it forever.

— *François Mauriac*

❧

Think of the biggest thing you can imagine.
Now double it.
I love you a hundred times that much!
— *Diane Ackerman*

❧

The sight of you...
is as necessary for me
as is the sun for the spring flowers.
— *Marguerite of Valois*

❧

It seemed to mean so little,
meant so much;
If only now I could recall that touch,
first touch of hand in hand.
— *Christina Rossetti*
(1830–1894) English poet

❧

Their priest was solitude, and they were wed:
And they were happy, forth their young eyes
Each was an angel, and earth paradise.
— *Lord Byron*
(1788–1824) English poet

❧

Have I loved before?
Such curiosity is vain.
And am I able to love?
Oh, allow me to demonstrate!
— *Adam Mickiewicz*
(1798-1855) Polish poet

❧

How helpless we are, like netting birds,
when we are caught by desire!
— *Belva Plain*

❧

I looked and saw your heart
In the shadow of your eyes...
— *unknown*

❧

One love is enough for a man.
— *Austin Dobson*

❧

I see you, though you will not look my way. You are
unaware that you handle the reins of my soul.
— *Anakreon of Theos*

❦

Every meeting is a marvelous pastime...
so when we happen to meet,
I greet you with a song in my heart.

— *Lorenz Hart*

❦

...how does love,
that fluttering thing,
set me wide and sure
as a hawk in the wing?

— *Mary Phelps*

❦

Whoever has loved
knows all that life contains
of sorrow and of joy.

— *George Sand*

❦

Lovely as those ladies were,
mine is a little lovelier.

— *e. e. cummings*
(1894-1962) *American poet*

❧

When you loved me,
I gave you the whole sun
and stars to play with...
and the volume of all the seas
in one impulse of your soul.
— *George Bernard Shaw*
(1856–1950) Irish dramatist

❧

I am weak from your loveliness.
— *John Betjeman*
(1906–1984) English poet

❧

Romance cannot be put
into quantity production—
the moment love becomes casual,
it becomes commonplace.
— *Frederick Lewis Allen*

❧

To the world you may be just one person.
To one person you may be the world.
— *unknown*

❧

Thought can never do the work of love.
> — *unknown*

❧

The moment my eyes fell on him,
I was content.
> — *Edith Wharton*
> *(1862-1937) American writer*

❧

There is no remedy for love
but to love more.
> — *Henry David Thoreau*
> *(1817-1862) American writer/philosopher*

❧

Kiss my soul through my lips.
> — *Lord Alfred Tennyson*
> *(1809-1892) English poet*

❧

Somewhere there waiteth in this world of ours
For one lone soul another lonely soul...
> — *Sir Edwin Arnold*
> *(1832-1904) English journalist*

❧

The most wonderful of all things in life,
I believe, is the discovery of another human being
with whom one's relationship has a glowing depth,
beauty and joy as the years increase.
This inner progressiveness of love between two
human beings is a most marvelous thing,
it cannot be found by looking for it or by
passionately wishing for it.
It is a sort of Divine accident.
— *Sir Hugh Seymour Walpole*
(1884-1941) English novelist

❧

I could do without many things with no hardship—
you are not one of them.
— *Ashleigh Brilliant*

❧

I wish I could remember that first day, first hour,
first moment of your meeting me.
— *Elizabeth Barrett Browning*
(1806-1861) English poet

❧

Love ends with hope.

— *Samuel Johnson*
(1709-1784) English poet/essayist

❧

There be none of Beauty's daughters
With a magic like thee;
And like music on the waters
Is thy sweet voice to me.

— *Lord Byron*
(1788-1824) English poet

❧

There is a garden in her face
Where roses and white lilies grow;
A heavenly paradise is that place
Wherein all pleasant fruits do flow.
There cherries grow which none may buy
Till "cherry-ripe" themselves do cry.

— *Thomas Campion*
(1567-1620) English poet/composer

❧

His heart runs away with his head.

— *George Colman the Younger*

❧

I long to talk with some old lover's ghost,
Who died before the god of love was born.
— *John Donne*
(1572–1631) English poet

❧

From their eyelids as they glanced dripped love.
— *Hesiod*
(8th century BC) Greek poet

❧

A hard beginning maketh a good ending.
— *John Heywood*
(1497–1580) English dramatist poet

❧

Some say that the age of chivalry is past,
that the spirit of romance is dead.
The age of chivalry is never past,
so long as there is a wrong
left unredressed on earth,
or a man or woman left to say,
I will redress that wrong,
or spend my life in the attempt.
— *Charles Kingsley*
(1819–1875) English poet

Second Marriage

❧

The married are those who have taken
the terrible risk of intimacy and, having taken it,
know life without intimacy to be impossible.
— *Carolyn Heilbrun*

❧

When widows exclaim loudly
against second marriages,
I would always lay a wager, that the man,
if not the wedding day,
is absolutely fixed on.
— *Henry Fielding*
(1707-1754) English novelist

❧

Marriage is the triumph
of imagination over intelligence.
Second marriage is the triumph
of hope over experience.
— *Samuel Johnson*
(1709-1784) English poet/essayist

❧

A man in love is incomplete until he has married—
then he's finished.

— *Zsa Zsa Gabor*
Hungarian actress

❧

It's pretty easy.
Just say 'I do' whenever anyone asks you a question.

— *Richard Curtis*

❧

Marriage is a reflection of who you are,
not what the world expects you to be.
This loving foundation gives the tranquil confidence
to speak boldly without a sound.

— *anonymous*

❧

Like everything which is not
the involuntary result of fleeting emotion
but the creation of time and will,
any marriage, happy or unhappy,
is infinitely more interesting
than any romance, however passionate.

— *W. H. Auden*
(1907-1973) English-born American poet

Strength

To love someone deeply gives you strength.
Being loved by someone deeply gives you courage.

— *Lao-tzu*
(604-531 BC) Chinese philosopher

Apparently I am going to marry Charles Lindbergh...
Don't wish me happiness—
it's gotten beyond that, somehow.
Wish me courage and strength
and a sense of humor—
I will need them all...

-- *Anne Morrow Lindbergh*
(1906-) American writer/aviator

For one human being to love another:
that is perhaps the most difficult of our tasks;
the ultimate, the last test and proof,
the work for which all other work is but preparation.

— *Rainer Maria Rilke*
(1875-1926) Austro-German poet

❧

Fate aids
the courageous.
— *Japanese proverb*

❧

Courage is the price that life exacts
for granting peace.
— *Amelia Earhart*
(1898-1937) American aviator

❧

You can't be brave if
you've only had wonderful things happen to you.
— *Mary Tyler Moore*
(1937-) American actress

❧

Reality is something you rise above.
— *Liza Minnelli*
(1946-) American entertainer

❧

When people keep telling you that you can't do a
thing, you kind of like to try it.
— *Margaret Chase Smith*

Success

❧

Many a man owes his success to his first wife
and his second wife to his success.
— *Jim Backus*
American actor

❧

Love one another and you will be happy.
It's as simple and as difficult as that.
— *Michael Leunig*

❧

With the catching end the pleasures of the chase.
— *Abraham Lincoln*
(1809-1865) 16th American president

❧

It's true that I did get the girl,
but then my grandfather always said,
"Even a blind chicken finds
a few grains of corn now and then."
— *Lyle Lovett*
American singer
upon marrying Julia Roberts, 1994

❧

Our greatest glory is not in never falling,
but in rising every time we fall.
— *Confucius*
(551-479 BC) Chinese philosopher

❧

Everything comes to him
who hustles while he waits.
— *Thomas Edison*
(1847-1931) American inventor

❧

The secrets of success are a good wife and a steady
job. My wife told me.
— *Howard Nemerov*

❧

The bottom line is that
(a) people are never perfect, but love can be,
(b) that is the one and only way that the mediocre
and vile can be transformed, and
(c) doing that makes it that.
We waste time looking for the perfect lover,
instead of creating the perfect love.
— *Tom Robbins*

❧

A man who has never made a woman angry
is a failure in life.
— *Christopher Morley*

❧

Neither a lofty degree of intelligence
nor imagination nor both together
go to the making of genius.
Love, love, love, that is the soul of genius.
— *Wolfgang Amadeus Mozart*
(1756-1791) Austrian composer

❧

It is easier to win love than to keep it.
— *Diane de Poitiers*

❧

Getting to know someone,
entering that new world,
is an ultimate, irretrievable leap into the unknown.
The prospect is terrifying.
The stakes are high, the emotions are overwhelming.
— *Eldridge Cleaver*

To improve is to change;
to be perfect is the change often.
— *Sir Winston Churchill*
(1874-1965) English prime minister

Never mistake motion for action.
— *Ernest Hemingway*
(1899-1961) American writer

He has half the deed done
who has made a beginning.
— *Horace*
(65-8 BC) Roman poet

To succeed in this world,
remember these three maxims:
to see is to know; to desire is to be able to;
to dare is to have.
— *Alfred de Musset*

Nothing succeeds like the appearance of success.
— *Christopher Lasch*

❧

Success: ninety-nine percent perspiration,
one percent inspiration.

— *anonymous*

❧

To achieve great things
we must live as though we were never going to die.
— *Marquis de Vauvenargues*

❧

Actions speak louder than words.
— *Dale Carnegie*
Motivational speaker/author

❧

A period of continuous bad luck is as improbable
as always staying on the straight path of virtue.
In both cases, there will eventually be a cure.
— *Charlie Chaplin*
(1889–1977) English film comedian/director

❧

One must be something
in order to do something.
— *Johann Wolfgang von Goethe*
(1749–1832) German poet/novelist

❧

If you want a place in the sun,
prepare to put up with a few blisters.
— *Abigail van Buren*
American advice columnist

❧

Show me a good loser,
and I'll show you a loser.
— *anonymous*

❧

The first law of holes:
when you're in a hole,
you have to stop digging.
—*Benjamin Franklin*
(1706–1790) American scientist/statesman

❧

Success is that old ABC—
ability, breaks and courage.
— *Charles Luckman*

❧

It takes twenty years
to become an overnight success.
— *Eddie Cantor*

❧

You cannot achieve great success
until you are faithful to yourself.
— *Friedrich W. Nietzsche*
(1844-1900) German philosopher

❧

Success is like dealing with your kid
or teaching your wife to drive.
Sooner or later you'll end up in the police station.
— *Fred Allen*

❧

The beginning is
the most important part of the work.
— *Horace*
(65-8 BC) Roman poet

❧

In any undertaking, two-thirds depends on reason,
one-third on chance.
Increase the first fraction and you are faint-hearted.
Increase the second and you are foolhardy.
— *Napoleon Bonaparte*
(1769-1821) French general/leader

ह৯

To climb steep hills
requires slow pace at first.
— *William Shakespeare*
(1564-1616) English writer

ह৯

Even a thousand-mile journey
Begins with the first step.
— *Japanese proverb*

ह৯

And throughout all Eternity
I forgive you, you forgive me.
— *William Blake*
(1757-1827) English poet/artist

ह৯

Even dust amassed
will grow into a mountain.
— *Japanese proverb*

ह৯

Success is simply a matter of luck.
Ask any failure.
— *Earl Wilson*

❧

Those who tell you it's tough at the top
have never been at the bottom.

— Joe Harvey

❧

It takes time to be a success,
but time is all it takes.

— anonymous

❧

The successful people
are the ones who think up things
for the rest of the world to keep busy at.

— Don Marquis
(1878-1937) American humorist poet

❧

Failures are like skinned knees —
painful, but superficial, they heal quickly.

— H. Ross Perot
American businessman

❧

You always pass failure on the way to success.

— Mickey Rooney
(1920-) American actor

❧

A dog that walks around
will find a stick.
— *Japanese proverb*

❧

Success seems to be largely a matter of hanging on
after others have let go.
— *William Feather*

❧

Fall down seven times
get up eight.
— *Japanese proverb*

❧

The man who wins may have been counted out
several times, but he didn't hear the referee.
— *H. E. Jansen*

❧

They gave each other a smile
with a future in it.
— *Ring Lardner*
(1885-1933) American short story writer/sports columnist

Success Proverbs

❧

Better poor with honor
than rich with shame.

❧

The busiest men find
the most leisure time

❧

He that labors and thrives,
spins gold.

❧

If you don't make mistakes
you don't make anything.

❧

Nothing succeeds
like success.

❧

Failure brings experience
and experience wisdom.

He who begins many things
finishes few.

If at first you don't succeed,
try, try again.

If a job's worth doing,
it's worth doing well.

I will win the horse
or lose the saddle.

Opportunity seldom
knocks twice.

Man learns little from success,
but much from failure.

❧

Payday comes
every day.

❧

Some men promise more in a day
than they fulfill in a year.

❧

The more you get,
the more you want.

❧

Those who climb high
often have a fall.

❧

What you lose on the swings
you gain on the roundabouts.

❧

Wealth is not his who makes it,
but his who enjoys it.

❧

Success has
many friends.

❧

Success makes a fool
seem wise.

❧

Sometimes the best gain
is to lose.

❧

The vulgar will keep no record of your hits,
only your misses.

❧

Any failure will tell you
success is nothing but luck.

❧

Success is best measured by how far you've come
with the talents you've been given.

Time

੨ৡ

In the blithe days of honeymoon,
With Kate's allurements smitten,
I lov'd her late, I lov'd her soon,
And call'd her dearest kitten.
But now my kitten's grown a cat,
And cross like other wives.
O! By my soul my honest Mat,
I fear she has nine lives.

— *James Boswell*
(1740–1795) Scottish biographer
Life of Samuel Johnson

੨ৡ

Love makes the time pass.
Time makes love pass.

— *French proverb*

੨ৡ

The story of a love is not important—
what is important is that one is capable of love.
It is perhaps the only glimpse
we are permitted of eternity.

— *Helen Hayes*
(1900–) American actress

❧

We study ourselves three weeks,
we love each other three months,
we squabble three years,
we tolerate each other thirty years,
and then the children start all over again.

— *Hippolyte Taine*
(1828-1893) French historian/philosopher

❧

Marriage from Love,
like vinegar from wine—
A sad, sour, sober beverage—
by time is sharpened from its high celestial flavour
down to a very homely household savour.

— *Lord Byron*
(1788-1824) English poet

❧

Enjoy every moment;
pleasures do not commonly
last so long as life.

— *Lord Chesterfield*
(1694-1773) English statesman

❧

Show wisdom.
Strain clear the wine;
and since life is brief, cut short far-reaching hopes!
Even while we speak, envious Time has sped.
Reap the harvest of today,
putting as little trust as may be in the morrow.

— *Horace*
(65-8 BC) Roman poet

❧

Do not put off till tomorrow
what can be enjoyed today.

— *Josh Billings*

❧

To live is so startling
it leaves little time for anything else.

— *Emily Dickinson*
(1830-1886) American poet

❧

Man's love is of man's life a thing apart,
'Tis woman's whole existence.

— *Lord Byron*
(1788-1824) English poet

Vision

When in doubt, make a fool of yourself.
There is a microscopically thin line
between being brilliantly creative
and acting like the most gigantic idiot on earth.
So what the hell, leap.
— *Cynthia Heimel*
Lower Manhattan Survival Tactics

Once the realization is accepted that even between
the closest human beings infinite distances continue
to exist, a wonderful living side by side can grow up,
if they succeed in loving the distance between them
which makes it possible for each to see each other
whole against the sky.
— *Rainer Maria Rilke*
(1875-1926) Austro-German poet

I have spread my dreams under your feet;
Tread softly because you tread on my dreams.
— *William Butler Yeats*
(1865-1939) Irish poet

❧

Go confidently in the direction of your dreams!
Live the life you've imagined!
As you simplify your life,
the laws of the universe will be simpler;
solitude will not be solitude,
poverty will not be poverty,
nor weakness weakness.
— *Henry David Thoreau*
(1817-1862) American writer/philosopher

❧

Ideals are like stars;
you will not succeed
in touching them with your hands.
But like seafaring man on the desert of waters,
you choose them as your guides,
and following them you will reach your destiny.
— *Carl Schulz*

❧

Imagination is more
important than knowledge.
— *Albert Einstein*
(1879-1955) American physicist

❧

We look forward to the time
when the power to love at will
replaces the love of power.
Then will our world know
the blessings of peace.
— *William Gladstone*
(1809-1898) Britain prime minister

❧

Ah, but a man's reach should exceed his grasp,
or what's a heaven for?
— *Robert Browning*
(1812-1889) English poet

❧

When people inquire I always just state,
"I have four nice children, and hope to have eight."
— *Aline Murray Kilmer*

❧

These times,
like all times,
are very good anew,
if we but know what to do with them.
— *Ralph Waldo Emerson*
(1803-1882) American writer

There are two worlds: the world that we can measure
with line and rule, and the world that we feel with
our hearts and imagination.

— *Leigh Hunt*
(1784-1859) English critic/essayist

I avoid looking forward or backward,
and try to keep looking upward.

— *Charlotte Brontë*
(1816-1855) English writer

We grow great by dreams.
All big men are dreamers.
They see things in the soft haze of a spring day
or the red fire of a long winter's evening.
Some of us let these great dreams die,
but others nourish and protect them,
nurse them through bad days
till they bring them to the sunshine and light
which comes always to those
who sincerely hope that their dreams will come true.

— *Woodrow Wilson*
(1856-1924) 28th American president

❦

One can never consent to creep
when one feels an impulse to soar.
— *Helen Keller*
(1880-1968) blind/deaf American writer

❦

When in doubt, jump!
— *Malcolm Forbes*

❦

There is a land of the living and a land of the dead
and the bridge is love,
the only survival, the only meaning.
— *Thorton Wilder*
(1897-) American novelist

❦

Every time a man puts
a new idea across
he finds ten men who
thought of it before he did—
but they only thought of it.
— *anonymous*

❧

Most people would succeed in small things
if they were not troubled with great ambitions.
— *Henry Wadsworth Longfellow*
(1807-1882) American poet

❧

The biggest things are always the easiest to do
because there is no competition.
— *William Van Horne*

❧

Ours is a world where people don't know what they
want and are willing to go through hell to get it.
— *Don Marquis*
(1878-1937) American humorist poet

❧

Fortune does not favor the sensitive among us:
it is the audacious, who are not afraid to say--
"The die is cast."
— *Desiderius Erasmus*
(1466-1536) Dutch humanist scholar

❧

No one knows what they can do till they try.
— *Publius Syrus*

❧

Fortune smiles on the audacious.

— *Virgil*
(70-19 BC) Roman poet

❧

Character equals destiny.

— *Heraclitus of Ephesus*
(500 BC) Greek philosopher

❧

Ideas won't keep;
something must be done about them.

— *Alfred North Whitehead*
(1861-1947) English philosopher

❧

There is a tide in the affairs of men,
Which, taken at the flood, leads on to fortune.

— *William Shakespeare*
(1564-1616) English writer

❧

He that will not when he may,
He shall not when he will.

— *Robert Mannyng*

❧

Discussion is the fruit of many men,
action the fruit of one.
— *Charles de Gaulle*
(1890-1970) French general/statesman

❧

Crank—a man with a new idea until it succeeds.
— *Mark Twain*
(1834-1910) American novelist

❧

With doubt and dismay you are smitten,
You think there's no chance for you, son?
Why the best books haven't been written,
The best race hasn't been run.
— *Berton Braley*

❧

Man's mind stretched to a new idea
never goes back to its original dimensions.
— *Oliver Wendell Holmes*
(1809-1894) American poet

❧

Where there is no vision, the people perish.
— *Proverbs 29:18*

❧

Imagination is the highest kite one can fly.
— *Lauren Bacall*
(1924-) American actress

❧

Don't let what you cannot do
interfere with what you can do.
— *John Wooden*

❧

Behold the turtle.
He makes progress only
when he sticks his neck out.
— *James B. Conant*
(1893-) American educator/chemist

❧

You see things that are and say, "Why?"
But I dream things that never were and say,
"Why not?"
— *George Bernard Shaw*
(1856-1950) Irish dramatist

Wife

❧

She rose to his requirement, dropped
The playthings of her life
To take the honorable work
Of woman and of wife.
— *Emily Dickinson*
(1830–1886) American poet

❧

A clever woman can turn a man into a lamb
in one moment
and convince him he's king of beasts the next.
— *Mary Jane Johnson*

❧

Advice on campaign behavior for first ladies:
Always be on time.
Do as little talking as humanly possible.
Remember to lean back in the parade
so everybody can see the president.
Be sure not to get too fat,
because you'll have to sit three in the back.
— *Eleanor Roosevelt*
(1884–) American first lady

❧

Instead of saying to a bride,
"Hold your husband,"...
we should say,
"Love your husband."
— *Margaret W. Jackson*

❧

For a wife that the daughter of a good mother.
— *Thomas Fuller*
(1608-1661) English clergyman/author

❧

When I lost my wife
every family in town offered me another.
— *American proverb*

❧

Wives are young men's mistresses,
companions for middle age,
and old men's nurses.
— *Sir Francis Bacon*
(1561-1626) English philosopher
Essays

&

In the choice of a horse and a wife,
a man must please himself,
ignoring the opinion and advice of friends.
— *George John Whyte-Melville*
Riding Recollections

&

My wife and I have a perfect understanding.
I don't try to run her life
and I don't try to run mine.

— *unknown*

&

A good wife always helps her husband
with the work around the house.

— *unknown*

&

I don't want to spend all of his money —
just most of it!

— *Cheryle Cummings*

&

Who so findeth a wife findeth a good thing...

— *Proverbs 18:22*

My wife doesn't care what I do when I'm away,
as long as I don't have a good time.
— *Lee Trevino*
Professional golfer

An ideal wife is any woman
who has an ideal husband.
— *Booth Tarkington*
(1869-1946) American novelist

Choose a wife by your ear than your eye.
— *Thomas Fuller*
(1608-1661) English clergyman/author

Do I love you? Haven't I shared your bed, washed
your shirts, made your meals for twenty-five years?
— *character, Golda*
Fiddler on the Roof

An ideal wife is one who remains faithful to you
but tries to be just as charming as if she weren't.
— *Sacha Guitry*
(1885-1957) French dramatist/actor

&

Wives are people who feel
they don't dance enough.

— *Groucho Marx*
(1891-1977) comedian

&

I believe in the difference between men and women.
In fact, I embrace the difference.

— *Elizabeth Taylor*
(1932-) American film actress

&

No matter how happily a woman may be married,
it always pleases her to discover
that there is a nice man
who wishes that she were not.

— *Henry Louis Mencken*
(1880-1956) American editor

&

There's only one way
to make a happy marriage,
and most wives
would like to know what it is.

— *anonymous*

Who follows his wife in everything
is an ignoramus.

— *Talmud*

Every man who is high up
likes to feel that he has done it all himself.
And the wife smiles and lets it go at that.
It's our only joke. Every woman knows that.

— *Sir James M. Barrie*
(1860-1937) Scottish dramatist/novelist

The world well tried—
the sweetest thing in life
is the unclouded welcome of a wife.

— *Nathaniel Parker Willis*
(1806-1867) American journalist

A woman will flirt with anybody in the world as
long as other people are looking on.

— *Oscar Wilde*
(1854-1900) Irish poet/essayist

Wisdom

We don't see things as they are.
We see them as we are.

— *Anaïs Nin*
(1903-1977) American writer

Love looks through a telescope;
envy, through a microscope.

— *Josh Billings*

Patience with others is Love,
Patience with self is Hope,
Patience with God is Faith.

— *Adel Bestavros*

I've sometimes thought of marrying,
and then I've thought again.

— *Noël Coward*
(1899-) English dramatist/actor

❧

Never, never, never,
never give up.
— *Sir Winston Churchill*
(1874-1965) English prime minister

❧

Honesty is the first chapter
in the book of wisdom.
— *Thomas Jefferson*
(1743-1826) 3rd American president

❧

More than kisses,
letters mingle souls.

— *John Donne*
(1572-1631) English poet

❧

Nobody, but nobody
can make it out here alone.
— *Maya Angelou*

❧

Jealousy is the only vice
that gives no pleasure.

— *anonymous*

෧

We cease loving ourselves
if no one loves us.

— *Germaine de Staël*
(1776–1817) French romance writer

෧

Ne'er take a wife till thou hast a house
(and a fire) to put her in.

— *Benjamin Franklin*
(1706–1790) American scientist/statesman

෧

The absolute yearning
of one human body for another particular body
and its indifference to substitutes
is one of life's major mysteries.

— *Iris Murdoch*
(1919–) Irish novelist/philosopher

෧

Two consciousnesses,
each dedicated to personal evolution,
can provide an extraordinary stimulus and challenge
to the other. Then ecstasy can become a way of life.

— *Nathaniel Branden*

❧

Love and stoplights can be cruel.
— *Sesame Street*

❧

Never marry for money.
Ye'll borrow it cheaper.
— *Scottish proverb*

❧

Never be possessive.
If a female friend lets on that she is
going out with another man,
be kind and understanding.
If she says she would like to go out
with the Dallas Cowboys,
including the coaching staff,
the same rule applies.
Tell her: "Kath, you just go right ahead
and do what you feel is right."
Unless you actually care for her,
in which case you must see to it
that she has no male contact whatsoever.
— *Bruce Jay Friedman*

Wishes & Desires

ε**ა**

If you knew I long for you.

ε**ა**

I wish I could paint the way I feel about you.

ε**ა**

I hope you love me.

ε**ა**

Please tell me something of your love

ε**ა**

I want to be with the woman I dream of.

ε**ა**

I need to see you, to caress you, to be with you.

ε**ა**

I am the person wanting you.

There is nothing in the world I want but you.

Please kiss me in your dreams.

You are close enough to hear my love from the heart.

You are life, sunshine,
music, and untold Fantasy.

There is poetry in my head and heart
since I have been in love with you.

I love you so deeply
my soul sings with pain and pleasure.

I send you the stars to wish upon.

Woman

Compromise:
An amiable arrangement
between husband and wife
whereby they agree
to let her have her own way.

— *anonymous*

A sweetheart is a bottle of wine,
a wife is a wine bottle.

— *Charles Pierre Baudelaire*
(1821–1867) French poet/critic

They had a dispute about
a night out with the boys.
But he finally decided to let her go.

— *anonymous*

A woman's whole life is a history of the affections.

— *Washington Irving*
(1783–1859) American essayist

A woman's life
can really be a succession of lives,
each revolving around some emotionally
compelling situation or challenge,
and each marked off
by some intense experience.
— *Wallis Warfield*
(1896-1986) Duchess of Windsor

There is nothing so wrong in this world
that a sensible woman can't set it right
in the course of an afternoon.
— *Jean Giraudoux*
(1882-1944) French novelist/playwright

It is a known fact that men are practical,
hardheaded realists, in contrast to women,
who are romantic dreamers
and actually believe that estrogenic skin cream
must do something
or they couldn't charge sixteen dollars
for that little tiny jar.
— *Jane Goodsell*

&

Every mother generally
hopes that her daughter
will snag a better husband
than she managed to do...
but she's certain that her boy
will never get as great a wife
as his father did.

— *anonymous*

&

If I were a girl, I'd despair.
The supply of good women far exceeds
that of the men who deserve them.

— *Robert Graves*
(1895–1985) English novelist/poet

&

A perfect Woman, nobly plann'd,
To warm to comfort, and command;
And yet a Spirit still and bright
With something of angelic light.

— *William Wordsworth*
(1770–1850) English poet

ক্ষ

No woman marries for money;
they are all clever enough,
before marrying a millionaire,
to fall in love with him first.

— *Cesare Pavese*

ক্ষ

When you see what some girls marry,
you realize how they must hate to work for a living.

— *Helen Rowland*

ক্ষ

The fickleness of the women I love
is only equalled by the infernal consistency
of the women who love me.

— *George Bernard Shaw*
(1856-1950) Irish dramatist

ক্ষ

Men marry because they are tired,
women because they are curious;
both are disappointed.

— *Oscar Wilde*
(1854-1900) Irish poet/essayist

❧

Some of us are becoming the men
we wanted to marry.

— *Gloria Steinem*
women's activist

❧

We in the industry know that behind every successful
screenwriter stands a woman.
And behind her stands his wife.

— *Groucho Marx*
(1891-1977) comedian

❧

Someone once asked me why women don't gamble
as much as men do and I gave the common sensical
reply that we don't have as much money. That was a
true but incomplete answer. In fact, women's
total instinct for gambling is satisfied by marriage.

— *Gloria Steinem*
women's activist

❧

Women and cats will do as they please.
Men and dogs had better get used to it.

— *Robert Heinlein*

ॐ

A woman is a miracle of divine contradictions.
— *Jules Michelet*
(1798-1909) English poet/novelist

ॐ

What is it that love does to women?
Without it she only sleeps;
with it alone, she lives.

— *Ouida*
(1839-1908) English novelist

ॐ

More marriages are ruined nowadays by the common
sense of the husband than by anything else.
How can a woman be expected to be happy with a
man who insists on treating her
as if she were a perfectly rational being?
— *Oscar Wilde*
(1854-1900) Irish poet/essayist

ॐ

Women are too imaginative and sensitive
to have much logic.
— *Mme. du Deffand*

❧

Every woman is the gift of a world to me.
— *Heinrich Heine*
(1797-1856) German Jewish poet

❧

A woman should never accept a lover
without the consent of her heart,
nor a husband
without the consent of her judgement.
— *Ninon de Lenclos*

❧

By the time you swear you're his,
shivering and sighing,
and he vows his passion is infinite,
undying—Lady, make a note of this:
one of you is lying!
— *The Toastmaster's Treasure Chest*

❧

Once made equal to man,
woman becomes his superior.
— *Socrates*
(469-399 BC) Greek philosopher

❧

Don't compromise yourself.
You are all you've got.

— *Betty Ford*
American first lady

❧

A woman's head is always influenced by her heart,
but a man's heart is always influenced by his head.

— *Countess of Blessington*

❧

A woman will always cherish
the memory of the man who wanted to marry her;
a man of the woman who didn't.

— *Viola Brothers Shore*

❧

Women are the glue that hold
our day-to-day world together.

— *Anna Quindlen*
American writer

❧

Don't accept rides from strange men—
and remember that all men are strange as hell.

— *Robin Morgan*

ॐ

Love, an episode in the life of man,
is the entire story of the life of a woman.
— *Germaine de Staël*
(1776-1817) French romance writer

ॐ

I do not believe women ever get sensible,
not even through prolonged association
with their husbands.
— *Dorothy L. Sayers*
(1893-1957) English writer

ॐ

A wise woman puts a grain of sugar
into everything she says to a man,
and takes a grain of salt
with everything he says to her.
— *Helen Rowland*

ॐ

The perfect mate,
despite what Cosmopolitan says,
does not exist,
no matter how many of those tests you take.
— *Suzanne Britt Jordan*

A woman must have money
and a room of her own.
— *Virginia Woolf*
(1882-1941) English writer

Nature has given women so much power
that the law has very wisely given them little.
— *Samuel Johnson*
(1709-1784) English poet/essayist

Women love always:
when earth slips from them,
they take refuge in heaven.
— *George Sand*
(1804-1876) French writer

Be bold in what you stand for
and careful what you fall for.
— *Ruth Boorstin*

❧

A liberated woman
is one who has sex before marriage
and a job after.

— *Gloria Steinem*
women's activist

❧

Woman inspires us to great things,
and prevents us from achieving them.

— *Alexandre Dumas*
(1802-1870) French novelist

❧

The great question...
which I have not been able to answer... is,
"What does a woman want?"

— *Sigmund Freud*
(1856-1939) Austrian psychoanalyst

❧

Who can find a virtuous woman?
for her price is far above rubies.
The heart of her husband doth safely trust in her.

— *Proverbs 31:10-11*

It is better to be the widow of a hero
than the wife of a coward.
— *Dolores Ibarruri*

A successful man is one
who makes more money than his wife can spend.
A successful woman is one
who can find such a man.
— *Lana Turner*
(1921-) American actress

A woman must be a genius
to create a good husband.
— *Honoré de Balzac*
(1799-1850) French novelist

Take a close-up of a woman past sixty.
You might as well use a picture
of a relief map of Ireland.
— *Lady Nancy Astor*
(1879-1964) English politician

❧

It is a waste of time
trying to charge a man's character.
You have to accept your husband as he is.
— *Queen Elizabeth II*
(1926-) Queen of Great Britian/Northern Ireland

❧

BRIDE: a woman with a fine prospect
of happiness behind her.
— *Ambrose Bierce*
(1842-1914) American satirist

❧

Women can do everything;
men can do the rest.

— *anonymous*

❧

Marriage, to women as to men, must be a luxury,
not a necessity; an incident of life, not all of it.
And the only possible way to accomplish this great
change is to accord to women equal power in the
making, shaping and controlling
of the circumstances of life.
— *Susan B. Anthony*

ॐ

Twenty years of romance
make a woman look like a ruin;
but twenty years of marriage
make her look like a public building.
— *Oscar Wilde*
(1854-1900) Irish poet/essayist

ॐ

Brigands demand your money or your life;
women require both.
— *Samuel Butler*
(1835-1902) English novelist

ॐ

Most women are not so young
as they are painted.
— *Sir Max Beerbohm*
(1872-1956) English essayist/satirist

ॐ

Woman would be more charming
if one could fall into her arms
without falling into her hands.
— *Ambrose Bierce*
(1842-1914) American satirist

❧

Housework is what a woman does that nobody
notices unless she hasn't done it.

— *Evan Esar*

❧

Never try to impress a woman,
because if you do,
she'll expect you to keep up the standard
for the rest of your life.

— *W. C. Fields*
American comedian

❧

One is not born a woman,
one becomes one.

— *Simone de Beauvoir*
(1908-1986) French writer/philosopher

❧

You have to admit that most women
who have done something with their lives
have been disliked by almost everyone.

— *Françoise Gilot*

૨☙

But if God had wanted us to think with our wombs,
why did He give us a brain?
— *Clare Boothe Luce*
(1903-) American playwright/diplomat

૨☙

One issue, at least,
men and women agree:
they both distrust women.
— *Henry Louis Mencken*
(1880-1956) American editor

૨☙

When a woman inclines to learning
there is usually something wrong
with her sexual apparatus.
— *Friedrich W. Nietzsche*
(1844-1900) German philosopher

૨☙

The average girl would rather
have beauty than brains
because she knows that
the average man can see much better
than he can think.
— *Ladies' Home Journal*

❧

Women are like elephants to me—
I like to look at 'em,
but I wouldn't want to own one.
— *W. C. Fields*
American comedian

❧

Women are like banks;
breaking and entering is a serious business.
— *Joe Orton*

❧

Most hierarchies were established by men
who now monopolize the upper levels,
thus depriving women of their rightful share
of opportunities to achieve incompetence.
— *Laurence J. Peter*

❧

The allurement that women hold out to men
is precisely the allurement that Cape Hatteras
holds out to sailors:
they are enormously dangerous and
hence enormously fascinating.
— *Henry Louis Mencken*
(1880-1956) American editor

❧

The charms of a passing woman
are usually in direct relation
to the speed of her passing.

— *Marcel Proust*
(1871-1922) French novelist

❧

There's nothing so similar
to one poodle dog
as another poodle dog,
and that goes for women, too.

— *Pablo Picasso*
(1881-1973) Spanish painter/sculptor

❧

The one point on which all women
are in furious secret rebellion
against the existing law
is the saddling of a right to a child
with the obligation to become
the servant of a man.

— *George Bernard Shaw*
(1856-1950) Irish dramatist

A woman without a man
is like a fish without a bicycle.
— *Gloria Steinem*
women's activist

Woman is like a teabag—
you can't tell how strong she is
until you put her in hot water.
— *Nancy Reagan*
American first lady

It is clearly absurd that it should be possible for
woman to qualify as a saint...
while she may not qualify as a curate.
— *Mary Stocks*

I hate women because
they always know where things are.
— *James Grover Thurber*
(1894-1961) American artist/author

❧

Whatever women do
they must do twice as well as men
to be thought half as good.
Luckily this is not difficult.

— *Charlotte Whitton*

❧

Women with "pasts" interest men
because men hope history will repeat itself.

— *Mae West*
(1892-1980) American actress

❧

A woman will always sacrifice herself
if you give her the opportunity.
It's her favorite form of self-sacrifice.

— *William Somerset Maugham*
(1874-) English writer

❧

My advice to the women's clubs of America
is to raise more hell and fewer dahlias.

— *William Allen White*
(1868-1944) American editor

૨ટ

The man who says his wife
can't take a joke,
forgets that she took him.

— *Oscar Wilde*
(1854-1900) Irish poet/essayist

૨ટ

The Eternal Feminine draws us upward.
— *Johann Wolfgang von Goethe*
(1749-1832) German poet/novelist

૨ટ

I expect that woman
will be the last thing
civilized by man.

— *George Meredith*
(1828-1909) English poet/novelist

૨ટ

Don't give a woman advice;
one should never give a woman anything
she can't wear in the evening.

— *Oscar Wilde*
(1854-1900) Irish poet/essayist

❧

The wife of a devil
grows worse than her mate.
— *Japanese proverb*

❧

Heav'n has no rage like love to hatred turn'd,
Nor hell a fury like a woman scorn'd.
— **William Congreve**
(1670-1729) English dramatist

❧

For the female of the species is more deadly
than the male.
— **Rudyard Kipling**
(1865-1936) English poet/writer

❧

God created woman.
And boredom did indeed cease
from that moment—
but many other things ceased as well.
Woman was God's second mistake.
— **Friedrich W. Nietzsche**
(1844-1900) German philosopher

෫෧

Prince, a precept I'd leave for you,
  Coined in Eden, existing yet:
Skit the parlor, and shun the zoo—
Women and elephants never forget.

— *Dorothy Parker*
(1893-) American satirist

෫෧

O woman! lovely woman!
Nature made thee to temper man:
we had been brutes without you.

— *Thomas Otway*
(1652-1685) English dramatist

෫෧

Scattered snowflakes
can't see white at all
in my wife's hair.

— *Japanese haiku*

෫෧

The only problem with women
is men.

— *Kathie Sarachild*

❧

A woman reading Playboy
feels a little like a Jew reading a Nazi manual.
— *Gloria Steinem*
women's activist

❧

It is assumed that the woman must wait,
motionless, until she is wooed.
That is how the spider waits for the fly.
— *George Bernard Shaw*
(1856–1950) Irish dramatist

❧

Many a happy marriage
is due to the fact that
they both are in love
with the same woman.

— *anonymous*

❧

A woman is a foreign land,
Of which, though there he settle young,
A man will ne'er quite understand
The customs, politics, and tongue.
— *Coventry Kersey Dighton Patmore*
(1823–1896) English poet/critic

&

Music and women I cannot give way to,
whatever my business is.

— *Samuel Pepys*

(1633-1703) English diarist

&

Social science affirms that a woman's place in society
marks the level of civilization.

— *Elizabeth Cady Stanton*

&

There is no realizable power that man cannot,
in time, fashion the tools to attain, nor any power so
secure that the naked ape will not abuse it.
So it is written in the genetic cards—
only physics and war keep him in check.
And the wife who wants him home by five,
of course.

— *Encyclopedia Apocryphia*

&

A woman has to be twice as good as a man
to go half as far.

— *Fannie Hurst*

❧

Being a woman is a terribly difficult trade,
since it consists primarily of dealing with men.

— *Joseph Conrad*
(1857-1924) English novelist

❧

Women prefer men who have
something tender about them—
especially the legal kind.

— *Kay Ingram*

❧

Women give us solace,
but if it were not for women
we should never need solace.

— *Don Herold*

❧

Anyone who says
he can see through women
is missing a lot.

— *Groucho Marx*
(1891-1977) American comedian

❧

There is nothing Madison Avenue can give us that
will make us more beautiful women. We are beautiful
because God created us that way.

— *Marianne Williamson*

❧

I married beneath me.
All women do.

— *Lady Nancy Astor*
(1879-1964) English politician

❧

Who loves not women,
wine and song,
Remains a fool
his whole life long.

— *Johann Heinrich Voss*

❧

A working girl is one
who quit her job to get married.

— *E. J. Kiefer*

Author Index

If you liked this book, you'll love this series:

Little Giant Book of Optical Illusions • Little Giant Book of "True" Ghost Stories • Little Giant Book of Whodunits • Little Giant Encyclopedia of Aromatherapy • Little Giant Encyclopedia of Baseball Quizzes • Little Giant Encyclopedia of Card & Magic Tricks • Little Giant Encyclopedia of Card Games • Little Giant Encyclopedia of Card Games Gift Set • Little Giant Encyclopedia of Dream Symbols • Little Giant Encyclopedia of Fortune Telling • Little Giant Encyclopedia of Gambling Games • Little Giant Encyclopedia of Games for One or Two • Little Giant Encyclopedia of Handwriting Analysis • Little Giant Encyclopedia of Home Remedies • Little Giant Encyclopedia of IQ Tests • Little Giant Encyclopedia of Logic Puzzles • Little Giant Encyclopedia of Magic • Little Giant Encyclopedia of Mazes • Little Giant Encyclopedia of Meditations & Blessings • Little Giant Encyclopedia of Names • Little Giant Encyclopedia of Natural Healing • Little Giant Encyclopedia of One-Liners • Little Giant Encyclopedia of Palmistry • Little Giant Encyclopedia of Puzzles • Little Giant Encyclopedia of Runes • Little Giant Encyclopedia of Spells & Magic • Little Giant Encyclopedia of Superstitions • Little Giant Encyclopedia of Toasts & Quotes • Little Giant Encyclopedia of Travel & Holiday Games • Little Giant Encyclopedia of UFOs • Little Giant Encyclopedia of Wedding Toasts • Little Giant Encyclopedia of Word Puzzles • Little Giant Encyclopedia of the Zodiac

Available at fine stores everywhere.